The Space of Culture

Critical Readings
in Hispanic Studies

Edited by
Stewart King & Jeff Browitt

Newark: University of Delaware Press

Monash Romance Studies

Monash Romance Studies is a series of refereed scholarly publications devoted to the study of any aspect of French, Italian and Spanish literature, language, culture and civilization. It will publish books and collections of essays on specific themes, and is open to scholars associated with academic institutions other than Monash.

Proposals for the series should be addressed to the general editor, from whom details of volumes previously published in the series are available:

Professor Brian Nelson
School of Languages, Cultures and Linguistics
Building 11
Monash University
Melbourne Vic. 3800
Australia.

Email: brian.nelson@arts.monash.edu.au

First American edition published 2004

Associated University Presses
2010 Eastpark Blvd
Cranbury, NJ 08512

ISBN   0 87413 917 1

Cataloguing-in-Publication Data is on file with the Library of Congress

Cover image: Lilit Thwaites

Design and layout: Caren Florance,
            *Letter*PRESS Design+Layout, Canberra
            letpress@webone.com.au
            www.webone.com.au/~letpress

The Space of Culture

Critical Readings in Hispanic Studies

We would like to thank Prof. Brian Nelson for his support and encouragement in the preparation of this collection. We would also like to thank the contributors for making this collection possible, especially Dr Lilit Thwaites, who kindly agreed to proof-read the manuscript.

We also thank Stuart Lees and John Tan for their invaluable technical assistance.

Contents

Introduction: the Space of Critique

Jeff Browitt

"I believe that the anxiety of our era has to do fundamentally with space"
(Foucault "Other Spaces" 23).

From the internal space of Gaston Bachelard's poetics and the "production" of urban space in the work of Henri Lefebvre, to Homi Bhabha's hybrid, "in-between" spaces of colonial resistance, to the postmodern geographies of Edward Soja and David Harvey, the spatial dimensions of human culture and sociality have increasingly come to the fore in critical theory in the second half of the twentieth century. By the late 1970s, Michel Foucault, conscious of the way the organisation and use of space "coded" social relations, had already proclaimed that a "whole history remains to be written of *spaces* – which would at the same time be the history of *powers* (both of these terms in the plural) – from the great strategies of geopolitics to the little tactics of the habitat" ("Eye" 149, emphasis in the original). For Foucault, "[s]pace is fundamental in any form of communal life; space is fundamental in any exercise of power" ("Knowledge" 252). In a further elaboration of this perceived need for a revalorisation of space vis-à-vis time, he declares:

> The great obsession of the nineteenth century was, as we know, history […]. The present epoch will perhaps be above all the epoch of space. We are in the epoch of simultaneity: we are in the epoch of juxtaposition, the epoch of the near and the far, of the side-by-side, of the dispersed. ("Other Spaces" 22)

Subsequently responding to Foucault's call to theorise space, Edward Soja also confronts the standard conception of modernity as primarily about a changed perception of time. For Soja, there is a need to challenge the hegemony of an "essentially historical epistemology" which dominates critical social theory and balances it against a "comparable critical sensibility to the spatiality of social life" ("History" 135). He thus calls for a critical theory that "re-entwines the making of history with the social production of space, with the construction and configuration of 'human geographies'" ("History" 137). Like Foucault, Soja takes issue with what he regards as an imperious, historicist paradigm in which space "still tends to be treated as fixed, dead, undialectical; time is richness, life, dialectic, the revealing context for critical social theorization" ("History" 137). In response to this paradigm Soja seeks "to give an additional twist to these options by defining historicism as an overdeveloped historical contextualization of social life and social theory that actively submerges and peripheralizes the geographical or spatial imagination" ("History" 140). In the introduction to his study *Thirdspace*, Soja thus invites the reader to "think differently about the meanings and significance of space and those related concepts that compose and comprise the inherent *spatiality of human life*: place, location, locality, landscape, environment, home, city, region, territory, and geography" (1, emphasis in the original).

Space becomes discursively constructed – described, categorised, rationalised, bound by laws, signposted – and this has a built-in indirect (and often direct) policing function for the control of social relations. In most situations, its effects are benign and linked to the need for a set of societal conventions capable of grounding mutual social recognition and boundary-setting. Yet such spatial control can just as easily be turned to more coercive ends: the panoptic surveillance of populations theorised by Foucault, strategic planning of towns and fortifications under colonial rule intended to re-centre native consciousness towards imperial domination, even the plans of modern housing designed to reflect the social distribution of space and function along gender and generational lines. Though Soja's work, like Foucault's, would seem to have its most appropriate application in studies in the design and use of urban space, it can also be usefully applied to the kinds of cultural analyses that concern us here.

A critical spatial imagination does not require us to opt for one space over another in an act of ideological dismissal – the settled space of traditional life (typically located in the country and romanticised as "natural") contrasted with the city space, often perceived as corrupt, violent, the site of racial and cultural mixing, as in the vexed issue of immigration. What seems more productive, rather than such stereotyping, is the clash of spatial conceptions and the ensuing negotiations in search of social stability. For the immigrant or refugee seeks social stability and continuity as much as the local who feels threatened by their presence. So too the regional minority encompassed by the nation-state and its homogenising drives. Local, regional and national spaces are interrelated to such a degree with the passage of time that the "Spanish" region of Catalonia, for instance, or the Basque Country, cannot presuppose the existence of clear geographical or cultural limits: both Spain and its regions blend into one another.

Mapping is often another means of control through spatialisation, but though professional cartography may mark out physical, spatial boundaries, what occurs within them – both socially and culturally – is a set of hetero-geneous and "impure" processes and practices:

> What lies behind the framework of political territories or formal ethnic regions are spatial constructs with deep ideological significance that may or may not correspond to political or formal constructs. These ideologies are forged in the territorial struggles that produce particular regional

arrangements and understandings and these in turn shape ideas, practices, activities and routines. (Murphy 29)

The notion of "autonomy", whether of the nation-state vis-à-vis globalisation or that of a region vis-à-vis the nation-state in which it is embedded, is hence largely a rhetorical gesture in our contemporary era. It is important for identity formation, but in the practical, real, material, social and cultural processes that animate our lives, impossible to achieve. Nevertheless, because geographical spaces are also the sites of struggle between the dominant and dominated orders, these material social and cultural processes of identity formation and cultural representation exhibit differential power relations. Indeed, it is often in the cultural realm where such unequal power relations manifest themselves most clearly – the control of representation. In the discourse of the state, where boundary-setting is meant to be definite and controlling, those spaces where quotidian culture seeks hedonistic pleasure or playful outlet – the voyeurism afforded by cinema and TV screen, the popular music event, carnival, the beach, even the bordello – are those zones where the dominant and dominated mix in hybrid border encounters. Spatial and thus symbolic and ideological orderings blur into each other. Spaces of state control – prison, psychiatric hospital, colony, and so forth – thus give way to alternative social spaces, orderings, knowledges and cultural practices.

In order to account for those spaces outside the conventional that might resist dominant paradigms, Foucault coined the term "heterotopia". Heterotopias are juxtaposed to the perfection and harmony of utopic space. They are heterogeneous spaces, "messy, ill constructed, and jumbled", which create an alternative space, "not of illusion, but of compensation" ("Other Spaces" 25). Though Foucault viewed many spaces as heterotopic – "museums and libraries, gardens and churches, brothels and theatres, prisons and barracks" ("Other Spaces" 27) – it is the space of the marginal, the subjugated, the dis-empowered, that provides a zone of disturbance, where cultural processes highlight the contradictions of society in a border region between the conventional and its other: "their presence either provides an unsettling of spatial relations or an alternative representation of spatial relations" (Hetherington 51). These "places of otherness" can thus represent "counter-sites" of contestation and convey a sense of incongruity and paradox, of socially transgressive practices:

> The main principle of heterotopias is that they bring together a collection of unusual things (or discursive statements), and give them a unity of meaning through the production of a space that acts symbolically as a site for the performance of an alternate mode of social ordering. Heterotopic relationships unsettle because they are out of place, their juxtaposition to a settled representation makes them appear anomalous and uncertain. (Hetherington 38)

Such marginal places can destabilise established orders of thinking and create "heterotopic anxiety" in societies of convention and control, provoking an often-predictable policing action. The discord between incommensurate objects in marginal or border spaces may involve the clash of tradition and modernity, imperial centre versus colonised periphery, the aging woman in the representational space reserved for youth, or the cinema in which alternative sexualities challenge a conservative moralism prescribed by the state, and these are a few of the themes pertinent to this collection of critical essays. But heterotopias are also sites of imagination, in which social contradictions might be negotiated. The otherness of Foucault's heterotopias is thus not the otherness of transcendence or autonomy, but rather that of possibility: the possibility of resisting or challenging hegemonic norms, of holding in dynamic tension the contradictions and contingencies of society. Indeed, such contradictions are fore-grounded in a space in which the veil is removed from conformist ideology to reveal the repression on which it is based.

Breaking with another kind of dualism, that of coloniser and colonised, Homi Bhabha theorises "third space" and "hybridity" as antidotes to such fixed and mutually exclusive binaries: "the importance of hybridity is not to be able to trace two original moments from which a third emerges, rather hybridity is to me the 'third space' which enables other positions to emerge" ("Third" 211). Drawing on Edward Said's understanding of the fantastic quality in Western constructions of the East, Bhabha drew attention to the fundamentally ambivalent operations of colonial stereotyping. If the overarching logic of colonial discourse was to "construe the colonized as a population of degenerate types on the basis of racial origin" (*Location* 70), it nonetheless also set up a fundamental split in the construction of otherness, which itself led to a peculiar ambivalence. Colonial discourse, wrote Bhabha, "produces the colonized as a social reality which is at once an 'other' and yet entirely knowable and visible" (*Location* 70–71). The result is a characteristic "in-betweenness" or "hybridity", greater than or at least different from the sum of its colonising and colonised parts. Insofar as the colonising power attempted to "reform" the subjectivity of its colonised subjects, what Bhabha calls colonial "mimicry" became central to the form of this hybridity: an "ironic compromise" between domination and difference, which produced an Other that is almost, but not quite the same. Mimicry is thus the sign of a "double articulation", according to Bhabha: "a complex strategy of reform, regulation and discipline, which 'appropriates' the Other as it visualizes power"; but also "the sign of the inappropriate [...] a difference or recalcitrance which coheres the dominant strategic function of colonial power, intensifies surveillance, and poses an immanent threat to [...] 'normalized' knowledges and disciplinary powers" (*Location* 86). Accordingly, the colonial encounter tends towards its own deconstruction as it turns "from *mimicry* – a difference that is almost nothing but not quite – to *menace* – a difference that is almost total but not quite" (*Location* 91, emphasis in the original). These dynamics are played out within the spatial logics of the very real, geographical and experiential space of the colonised.

From a similarly inspired postcolonial perspective, the Brazilian cultural critics, Silviano Santiago and Renato Ortiz, theorise the ambivalent "space in-between" (Santiago) and "the other territory" of postcoloniality and its intellectual discourse, where the national and the cosmopolitan uncomfortably combine. Signifying practices may be generated within a determined space (geographical, symbolic or theoretical), but they may be received in entirely different ones. What happens to these practices when they move to another space has been a concern, among others, of reception theory. Yet reception theory has never really engaged with the issue of intellectual reception in a space (for example, the postcolonial nation) in which outside ideas and traditions are meant by dominant colonial powers to be understood, acknowledged and accepted as originally conceived, but are just as often rejected, parodied, mimicked or subverted. The production and reproduction of intellectual discourse therefore occurs not only through time and through human interrelations, but also and importantly within certain spatial coordinates and arrangements and not in others, and this has implications: "what is affirmed [in Santiago's work] is the value of a text of the colonized culture as space in-between, which retroactively affects the text of the dominant culture, thus creating the possibility of a concrete evaluation of the universality of the texts of the metropolis" (Gazzola and Melo Miranda 3).

We become socialised and acculturated within a determined space, even if the cultural messages and images we receive come from outside that territory. Indeed, it is the very negotiation of culture from outside one's lived communal space that is at issue for diasporic populations (the immigrant, the displaced, the exile). But though we are accustomed to the idea of cultures being rooted in a defined physical territory, mass media, modern transportation, migration, the global circulation of cultural goods and symbols, the transnationalisation of urban planning, and so forth "deterritorialise" cultures and processes of cultural identity formation such that identities are no longer exclusively localisable in a specific geographical space, but are amalgams of local identities and memories with global popular cultural processes and artefacts in what can only be described as a hybrid, deterritorialised space for the formation of subjectivity and identity. This problematises simplistic appeals to idealised, local, "authentic" cultures (Ortiz 30).

This compilation of essays can be viewed as one in which space is employed as an operational concept, not only in its real-geographical sense, but in its metaphorical, theoretical and discursive manifestations, along with the related notions of the visible/invisible, dominant/dominated, empowered/powerless. The cultural analyses of space range from colonial domination (King) and international struggles over territorial claims (Foster), to a meditation on the politics of location (Browitt), to the issue of spatial representation of mature-age women (Thwaites) and gay men (Martínez Expósito) within a dialectic of visibility/invisibility in Spanish theatre and cinema. It is no surprise that the first three are concerned with the heterosexual, male dominated space of statist, macro-political issues, and the latter with micro-spatial and affective relations in the spheres of gender and sexual politics, relations in which subordinate cultures attempt to wrest a space of representation from within the interstices of power. Space also becomes a dimension of imagination and "compensation" in Argentina, in the soundscapes in which the tango becomes metaphor for the failures of Argentine modernity (Bendrups; Anad), and the hybrid, discursive space of the quasi-fictional, journalistic exposé in contemporary Argentine politics (Hortiguera).

Alfredo Martínez Expósito examines one of the most popular films of the Spanish sex comedy genre, the 1970 *No desearás al vecino del quinto*, and reads it against the grain of most traditional criticism which sees in its portrayal of homosexuality only "reactionary social and moral values". For Martínez Expósito, while the film's plot is acted out against a familiar stereotypical landscape – a promiscuous and modernising Madrid counterposed to the "decent" values of rural tradition – it paradoxically gives representational space to a stigmatised minority within a homophobic milieu. Visibility is nevertheless a mixed blessing: it can lead to familiarity and thus knowledge, but also to the perpetuation of stereotypes. The film thus has historical-testimonial value, as it highlighted the limits of the permissible and served as a fictional vehicle for the sublimated sexual anxieties of the audience itself beneath the gaze of a patriarchal and reactionary state.

Lilit Thwaites's article appraises the work of Pilar Pombo, a Spanish female playwright, in the context of the emergence of a distinctly woman-centred theatre in post-Franco Spain. Pombo's works foreground the plight of those who could be regarded as the doubly-marginalised: "everyday women [...] who struggle to make a living and/or simply survive" and their virtual invisibility in contemporary Spanish society. In Pombo's plays the space of visibility is also a space of discourse, as centrality is yielded to "a distinctly female discourse with a woman-centred focus", reversing the gaze of the traditionally male-centred control of cultural representation. Thwaites shows how the portrayal of a range of women, from the young, working-class to elderly pensioners, reveal resilience, humour and strategies of survival as the (mis)fortunes of these women are played out against a background of a modernising and increasingly selfish society.

For Foucault, brothels and colonies are two extreme types of heterotopia ("Other Spaces" 27), and their primordial functions, one might add, are not too dissimilar. They are typically sites where the dominant exercise power over the abjected and subordinated other. The organisation of colonial space is both functional and symbolic – it serves to control populations and its fortresses, prisons, seats of administrative power and its regimes of representation act as a warning. Foucault theorised the disciplinary power exercised through spatial organisation, most notoriously in Bentham's model surveillance design for prisons in the Panopticon. It takes little license to view Spain as a national space within which regional cultural and political formations are disciplined and rationalised within the panoptic gaze of a centralising Madrid, both during the fascist phase of state power under Franco and since. Culture and geography have been absolutely central to this struggle. The sanctity of national space and Catholicism combine in the attempted production in Francoist Spain of a homogenised cultural space free from the pollutions of alternative traditions and languages that threaten the body of the nation. Franco's dictatorship could be seen as one of the last attempts in the twentieth century to halt modernity in its tracks, at least its secular, socially and politically modernising variant, which threatened to overturn Castile's conservative, centrist and homogenising conception of national community.

In this volume, Stewart King brings postcolonial critique and the concept of "internal colonialism" to an analysis of the problematic relationship between the centralising Spanish State and one of its recalcitrant regions – Catalonia – through a reading of a series of representative Catalan novels and their ability to generate alternative understandings of history. King highlights how narratives forged from within Catalan identity politics and issues of cultural representation bear witness to "struggles for the control of geographic and social spaces". The domination of Catalonia accords with Antonio Gramsci's concept of hegemony: the threat of physical coercion is combined with the attempt to permeate throughout the whole of society a system of values and beliefs supportive of the ruling power. Such hegemony necessarily involves the attempted control of representation and history and the principal vehicle for such domination has been the Spanish language itself. Hence resistance takes as its point of departure the Catalan language and a revisionist history. Nevertheless, King is wary of simplistic either/or oppositions – centre/periphery, Spain/Catalonia – since Catalan nationalism often harbours its own exclusions and blindnesses.

Wars of physical aggression are inevitably accompanied on the ideological level by propaganda. Kevin Foster picks his way through the negative representations of Argentinians during the Falkland Islands/ Malvinas war in the early 1980s as the British press engaged a now familiar stereotypical dichotomy: "civilised" Europeans versus "barbaric" Latinos. His article explores the anxiety of a post-empire Britain still gravely concerned with geographical "integrity" and identity. Though such a sense of integrity absurdly encompasses the Falkland Islands in the distant South Atlantic, it is nevertheless the symbolic spatial unity of empire, an imagined community of purpose and culture, which is perceived to be under threat. The spatial conditions of disorder – the geographical disorder threatened by the Argentinian invasion of the Falklands Islands/Malvinas – triggers a psychological disorder in the metropolitan power which results in a perceived loss of self-esteem. The war thus involved a perceived need on the part of a major European power, still trading on the (in)glories of the colonial past, to reconfirm an imperial narrative based on a conception of moral and cultural superiority of the European coloniser over the non-European other. The geographical landscape of the Falklands Islands/Malvinas thus becomes a moral landscape as the concepts of development and backwardness are mapped onto geographical space setting up a regime of valuing in which the peripheral, "backward", non-metropolitan centre can never be accorded any, or precious few, positive attributes.

For his part, Jeff Browitt contemplates theoretical space, "*loci* of enunciation" and the issue of intellectual colonisation in contemporary debates within Latin American cultural studies and the role and acceptance/ rejection of the work of non-Latin American intellectuals. Browitt engages with these divisive debates in an effort to detect common ground from which such debates might be defused and pushed in a more constructive direction. In Browitt's opinion, the accusations of intellectual imperialism levelled at non-Latin American Latin Americanists seems to relate to a narrow conception of intellectual propriety and commitment: one can only really be authentic if one grounds one's reflections in geography, in a territory that one intimately knows from lived experience. According to this conception, if one is outside "native" space, one's engagements with the cultural politics of a national space other than one's own necessarily involves blindness. While the role of the deracinated, "free-floating", postmodern travelling intellectual, without any organic ties with a specific community is rightly criticised within some Latin Americanist intellectual circles, for some it is a false charge directed at those who have merely chosen to work in a particular field rather than some other. Acknowledging that the lack of daily familiarity with cultural experience that is not one's own imposes certain limitations, Browitt points out that nonetheless no intellectual space is uncontaminated from outside influence, especially within a zone that has had on-going contact with Europe and North America for over 500 years, and that the Latin American intellectual is already in a theoretical and ideological "space in between" (Bhabha "Third", Santiago, Ortiz). Browitt finds in a suitably modified version of Raymond Williams's cultural studies, a possible model and point of reconciliation.

Faye Bendrups reflects on the nexus between experience, place and failed aspirations in the lyrics of the Argentine tango: the overall feeling of sadness that attaches to this most singular of musical forms. For Bendrups, the tango space has a dual geographical origin: the isolation of the unforgiving interior and the precariousness of existence in the bustling urban space of Buenos Aires. She links both through an analysis of themes of "grief and loss". While the tango is primordially attached to Buenos Aires in most people's imagination, Bendrups is concerned to highlight the less obvious connection to the interior. Here too, and since colonial times, "the spatial logic of such a void" – the vastness and inhospitality of the Pampa and the littoral – has contributed to a sense of loss and abandonment. The tango space thus becomes a mythical, heterotopic space outside the modernising and expanding nation, a space of nostalgia and consolation. Similarly, the harshness of the interior is mirrored in the mushrooming city, with its tales of unrequited love and unrealised dreams. The tango form thus functions as a window onto Argentina's problematic relationship with modernity and progress. Yet what one notices is the tango's potential for re-framing: the tango as a space of possibility. As a "psychical geography", onto its form can be mapped the most contemporary of personal and collective issues.

Whereas in Bendrups the focus centres on the tango space of failed dreams and aspirations, the underlying presence of tango in Julio Cortázar's literary production is the theme of Guillermo Anad's essay. Anad proposes to fill a void in scholarship dealing with Julio Cortázar's literary production: his tango-inspired poetry. For Anad, Cortázar's poetry is the most neglected genre in his oeuvre, yet it is perhaps the one that most reflects his problematic relationship with his homeland during the first Peronist government. Here, the discursive space of the tango lyric becomes a vehicle for a much more intimate and nostalgic Cortázar, meditating not only on themes of "absence and abandonment", but also on issues of social injustice.

The volume closes with Hugo Hortiguera's ruminations on the material spatiality of a popular linguistic practice in contemporary Argentina: the documentary story of the lives of the rich and powerful. Hortiguera likens these stories to the French *potin*, a hybrid genre that trades in "pseudo-information", a blend of fact and fiction in which political scandal is presented as entertainment and in which the discursive space of an ostensibly objective, journalistic exposé is contaminated by the stylistic conventions of soap opera, melodrama and gossip. The Argentine *potin* of the 1990s centres on a celebrity (political or otherwise) who stands in, metonymically, for the comic intrigues of national affairs. Hortiguera combines discourse analysis with semiotic readings of book-covers, which in their photographic-spatial constructions, mimic the tawdry lives of their central characters. Here, different and juxtaposed discourses jostle and collide "in an ambiguous and hybrid space", highlighting the contradictions of the most unsavoury dimension of Argentine political culture in the 1990s: the political machinations and private *peccadillos* of the then president, Carlos Menem and his young and glamorous Chilean bride, Cecilia Bolocco. For Hortiguera, such public discourse is so filled with kitsch detail, rumour, innuendo, ironic narrative asides and so forth, that it becomes virtually empty, filling with "noise" a dysfunctional civil society, a collapsing, peripheral player within capitalist globalisation.

Art and critique in solidarity with the marginal can create shifting and hybridised boundaries of the acceptable, liminal or heterotopic spaces in which different, often opposed, moral communities can intersect in a less threatening environment in which they can metaphorically "converse", thus opening up the possibility of, if not reconciliation, at least acknowledgement of the other's existence. Therefore, though frequently a site of abjection, the heterotopic margin can also be a space "where we move in solidarity to erase the category colonizer/colonized. Marginality is the space of resistance" (hooks 152). Indeed, if we accept the premise that identities are not innate or essential but relational, malleable, formed within the play of difference and dialogue, then the critical representation of the interaction of differing moral communities in space merely makes explicit that which already obtains. Crucially, though, rather than merely "reflecting" or bearing witness to such interactive contexts of identity formation and moral boundary-setting, artistic and critical representation often actively *create* them and thus become important in changing societal attitudes. Cinema, for instance, may merely reinforce and perpetuate prejudices, but so too may it help to expose and thus destroy them. Since reception theory, we are accustomed to understanding that symbolic messages are often consumed in unforeseen and unpredictable ways. When marginality is performed, it consequently becomes visible and this alone can often be a form, albeit non-revolutionary, of empowerment and knowledge creation.

Heterotopias may reproduce social space and its dominant structures, or they may challenge and reorder it. The mere fact of spatiality juxtaposing incommensurate elements – the marginal in the media on their own terms; the colonised occupying the seat of power; the radical critic in the space of public discourse – effects a dissonant tension within social conventions, threatening to bring down established hierarchies. And so we return to the space of critical discourse and this collection of soundings in Hispanic literary and cultural studies, in which art and critique become spaces of resistance and possibility, heterotopic sites in which the space of convention, stasis and control cedes to the space of reflection, movement and liberation.

Works cited

Bhabha, Homi. "The Third Space: Interview with Homi Bhabha." *Identity, Community, Culture, Difference.* Ed. Jonathon Rutherford. London: Lawrence & Wishart, 1990. 207–21.

——. *The Location of Culture.* Routledge, London, 1994.

Foucault, Michel. "The Eye of Power." *Power/Knowledge: Selected Interviews and Other Writings 1972–1977.* New York: Pantheon, 1980. 146–65.

——. "Space, Knowledge, and Power." *The Foucault Reader.* Ed. Paul Rabinow. London: Penguin, 1984. 239–56.

——. "Of Other Spaces." *Diacritics* 16 (1986): 22–27

Gazzola, Ana Lucía, and Wander Melo Miranda. "Introduction: Silviano Santiago: A Voice In-Between." *Santiago* 1–8.

Hetherington, Kevin. "Identity Formation, Space and Social Centrality." *Theory, Culture & Society* 13.4 (1996): 33–52.

hooks, bell. *Yearning: Race, Gender and Cultural Politics.* Boston: South End Press, 1990.

Murphy, Alexander B. "Regions As Social Constructs." *Progress in Human Geography* 15 (1991): 23–35.

Ortiz, Renato. *Otro territorio: ensayos sobre el mundo contemporáneo.* Bogotá: Convenio Andrés Bello, 1998.

Santiago, Silviano. *The Space In-Between: Essays On Latin American Culture.* Durham, NC: Duke University Press, 2001.

Soja, Edward W. "History: Geography: Modernity." *The Cultural Studies Reader.* Ed. Simon During. London & New York: Routledge, 1993.135–50.

——. *Thirdspace: Journeys to Los Angeles and Other Real-and-Imagined Places.* Oxford: Blackwell, 1996.

Visibility and Performance in the Anti-Gay Sexy Spanish Comedy: No desearás al vecino del quinto (1970)[1]

Alfredo Martínez-Expósito

No desearás al vecino del quinto (1970) is the most representative of a highly idiosyncratic comedy genre that flourished in Spanish cinema in the last years of the Franco regime. Neither the movie nor the genre at large has attracted much critical attention outside Spain (Jordan), due in part to the fact that, being intended for a domestic market, they were rarely exported, and in part to their very low cinematic quality. As most Spanish critics noted, the sexy *comedia a la española* was financially successful thanks to a combination of low production budgets and huge box-office returns, but it also set new standards of bad taste and contributed to the perpetuation of the reactionary social and moral values of Francoism. *No desearás al vecino del quinto*[2] has been frequently dismissed as typical of this deplorable genre, and sometimes as an inconsequential comedy whose only merit was the unprecedented popularity reached by leading actor Alfredo Landa in his impersonation of an effeminate couturier. However, this movie ranked as the most profitable in the history of Spanish film before Almodóvar's 1988 hit *Mujeres al borde de un ataque de nervios*. The movie certainly was one of the big hits of the early seventies (it opened in Madrid in October 1970, in Barcelona in February 1971, and then in all other Spanish major cities).[3] Official figures show box office receipts of 177.5 million pesetas and more than 4 million tickets sold; to that should be added the benefits from the videotape editions such as the one published in 1993 by CIC in the series "Gran Comedia Española".[4] These figures compare extremely well with the more politically serious and intellectually respectable films of the period; Carlos Saura's *El jardín de las delicias* (1970), for instance, made only 12 million pesetas.[5]

No desearás al vecino del quinto, on the other hand, was the first mainstream Spanish movie of the Franco era to offer a consistent study of the representation of a gay man. Carlos Arévalo's *¡Harka!* (1941) and Juan de Orduña's *¡A mí la legión!* (1942), have inspired queer readings of the close relationship of the two main characters within a military context, and these have certainly become key titles of the Spanish gay canon. But by no means can it be argued that the homosexual content is unambiguous in a military narrative of camaraderie and mateship. The first unambiguously gay character of post-war Spanish film appeared in the 1961 musical *Diferente*, a snobbish, obscure film officially directed by Luis María Delgado but effectively managed and designed by Argentinian dancer Alfredo Alaría, who played the main character – a gay dancer at odds with his family and with his upper social class background. Curiously enough, this highly subversive movie passed censorship the same year Buñuel's *Viridiana* was banned in Spain after being branded as blasphemous by *L'Osservatore Romano*.[6] If *Diferente* showed a difficult allegoric language to mitigate its overtly gay-voice narrative, *No desearás al vecino del quinto* displayed an easy and unashamed heterosexist approach to homosexuality.

The alignment of commercial success and homosexual representation is somehow disconcerting in the extremely homophobic environment of fascist Spain. Indeed, one of the recurring questions in the reviews I have been able to read concerns precisely the reason for the movie's striking popular success, which some critics feared would be in some way or another linked to its obvious homophobic façade. Although some queer critics have dismissed the movie as a silly version of popular homophobia (Mira Nouselles) it is clear, from today's perspective, that the derogatory and ridiculous representation of the homosexual in *No desearás al vecino del quinto* was nevertheless a representation of homosexuality in a time when such representations were strictly banned by official censorship. It is also clear that the massive popularity of its gay character set the visual standards for homosexuality in subsequent mainstream representations of gay men. From today's perspective it is also hard to believe that this movie dared to create a main character who was homosexual without its being banned by the Censorship Committee.[7]

The film is interesting for other reasons too. Antón, the homosexual, for instance, turns out to be a false homosexual – he simply pretends to be gay so that the husbands, fathers, brothers and boyfriends of his small-town clients perceive him as an inoffensive unmanly man, incapable of threatening their honour in the fitting room. Rather than a "degenerate", the couturier is a promiscuous heterosexual who derives great voyeuristic pleasures from his job in provincial Toledo while giving free rein to his baser instincts during his monthly predatory visits to Madrid. Promiscuity, as the main enemy of Catholic family values, was the censors' *bête noire*, but it was also the golden dream of many sexually repressed male Spaniards of the time. The main feature of the sexy Spanish comedy was precisely this tension between the dreams of the (male) audience and the traumas of their official repression. The plot of *No desearás al vecino del quinto*, rich in instances of that tension, carefully avoided censorship[8] by denying everything it was proposing, by using the old comic conventions of misunderstanding and false assumptions.[9] In the movie, the fact that none of the characters is ultimately gay does not prevent the audience from pondering the possibility that two of them – not just one! – could be. Apart from the couturier, who is believed to be gay because of the stereotypical qualities evident in his *mise-en-scène*, featuring overtly camp clothes, gestures and high pitched voice, his neighbour, a good-looking gynaecologist called Pedro, will be percieved to have become gay when his fiancée and his mother find him sharing an apartment with the couturier in Madrid. Thus, in a genre most commonly associated with the exhibition of female bodies through a masculine gaze, *No desearás al vecino del quinto* dared to exhibit seemingly homosexual men through a feminine gaze.

Looking beyond its technical flaws and the insufferable vulgarity of its retrograde jokes, this particular film poses interesting questions about the conditions of possibility of homosexual representation in a homophobic milieu, and it does so through a surprisingly clever use of two important devices in the representation of (gay) identity – visibility and performance.

Visibility and performance

DOCTOR: ¿Qué tiene que ver el tal Antón con su Pedro? No veo la
relación.

JACINTA: Usted no la ve. Pero la relación existe. ¡Vaya si existe!

Visibility is a key political issue in the agendas of lesbian and gay liberationists, as it was earlier for feminists and women's liberation activists. Visibility would become the necessary complement to pride in the self-assertive discourses against the closet and the politics of silence. As Rosemary Hennessy puts it,

> For a lesbian and gay political project that has had to combat the heteronormative tyranny of the empirical in order to claim a public existence at all, how visibility is conceptualized matters. Like "queer", "visibility" is a struggle term in gay and lesbian circles now – for some simply a matter of display, for others the effect of discourses or of complex social conditions. (Hennessy 31)

In Spain, however, it would seem that the politics of the visible has played a rather modest role in the gay and lesbian movement, and has found only belated – and limited – recognition in mainstream media (Aliaga; Aliaga and Cortés; Llamas; Mira Nouselles). Most Spanish reactions to the politics of visibility do mention the unwelcome confrontational rhetoric that seems to be an inherent part of it. Rendering homosexuality visible is, in itself, a transgressive political operation that subverts several of the defining principles of patriarchy: heteronormativity, homosexual taboo, and the heterosexual monopoly of the symbolic order. The capacity of queer discourses to render homosexuality intelligible is particularly relevant in times or places where homosexual traditions have been silenced for long periods and where social memories of lesbians and gay men have been suppressed. The erasure of all signs of homosexuality has the insidious effect of preventing homosexuals from using those texts as mirrors where their own sexuality might become readily apparent. There is now ample evidence that in societies where representations of homosexuals and homosexuality are banned, lesbians and gay men can establish reverse identity links with negative representations of homosexuality (Cleminson; Dynes; Mirabet i Mullol; Smith). Paradoxically, the less visible homosexuality is forced to be, the more useful its traces become.

The politics of visibility has affected gay men's and lesbians' self-perceptions, as well as the way homosexuality is portrayed in mainstream media. Although there can be little doubt that most of the changes have been positive, it is also true that homosexual visibility has been appropriated by unlikely agents. Hennessy interestingly shows how large corporations make use of commodified homosexual icons in their advertising campaigns in order to convey a progressive and "cool" image, while at the same time exploiting their underpaid, overworked employees in third-world countries. Gay-friendly advertising has indeed become a major source of stereotyping that has greatly contributed to concealing images of poor, non-white, older, rural, sick, handicapped, and otherwise "unfashionable" images of lesbians and gay men. Despite the abuses of capitalism, however, visibility remains one of the main strategies of queer liberationists. Our recent historical experience seems to endorse the axiomatic belief of earlier activists that a higher level in the social presence of homosexuals would be followed by a higher level of tolerance, acceptance and integration.

Many queer theorists have been careful to avoid the reductionist use of visibility that has become topical among media commentators, and that centres the whole issue on a positivist notion of the visible. Judith Butler is perhaps more direct than others when she points out that visibility is not only about bodies or public personae, but also – and primarily – about discourses, semiotic processes, modes of intelligibility (Butler). In short, about knowledge. Thus, the coming-out narrative, which is always a process of rendering visible what previously was hidden or disguised, is important because it provokes or invokes a kind of paradigm, discourse or meta-narrative. The saying "out of sight, out of mind" – whose Spanish equivalent, "ojos que no ven, corazón que no siente", puts the emphasis on emotions – is a popular way of linking visibility and thinking, or invisibility and the collapse of understanding. Butler's argument implies that political agendas based on visibility do, after all, target social processes of semiosis, and not, as was commonly believed not so long ago, the agents of those processes, i.e. lesbians and gay men that rendered their sexuality visible and viewers or spectators of those "outings". When 1970 audiences of *No desearás al vecino del quinto* were confronted with extremely unusual images of homosexuals and their relatives who were concerned for them, those audiences were undoubtedly confronted with homosexuality itself.

The politics of visibility is frequently based on the rhetoric of showing. A large portion of queer theory has been devoted to the nature of everyday staging of socio-sexual behaviour and to the performative nature of identity construction (Butler; Parker and Sedgwick). Both essentialist and constructivist arguments about the nature of identity performance offer interesting clues for the understanding of drag and effeminacy, which in the seventies and early eighties were the main expressions of male homosexuality in Spanish culture.

A point of disagreement between radical and assimilationist queer activists remains the normalising effects of visibility: while radicals generally advocate for a thorough transformation of society through an increased exposure of its queer elements, assimilationists aspire to reduce the tensions produced by homophobia. Strategies based on visibility and the gay gaze do feature prominently in both agendas. Queering and normalising, although dramatically different in rituals and rhetoric, might be the two sides of just one single attempt to replace patriarchal codes of socio-sexual behaviour with a new set of more plural, diverse and inclusive norms. To this end, queer activists and intellectuals have busied themselves with the onerous task of actually drafting norms and codes, hoping that capitalist structures will propagate them in a positive light. Capitalist structures, however, are more permeable to the naturalising effects of visibility and the gay gaze than one might have imagined because it is by virtue of the double process of domestication and validation that the homosexual becomes a commodity. Advertising campaigns based on gay icons, which are only possible in media environments already exposed to homosexual visibility, attract new customers and set out to flatter the sensibilities of lesbians and gay men. Yet, this comes at a price: the power of deciding what forms of homosexuality are suitable and how they should be marketed is no longer in the hands of lesbians and gays. Corporate power, usually associated with the instances of power that regulate social and sexual life, might be regarded with growing unease by those queer intellectuals who would be happier if capitalist interests were left out of the regulation of sexuality. (After all, why should Atlántida Films and Fida Cinematografica have ethical concerns about the consequences of their portrayal of male homosexuality in *No desearás al vecino del quinto?*)

An important chapter in the process of domestication and validation of homosexuality is the academic activity of queer critics. A queer reading of a cultural product is in itself a normalising exercise. A queer rendering of a homophobic text of the past might contribute not only to normalise homosexuality, but also to identify the set of conventions that perpetuated homophobia in different historical periods. In this sense, the strategy of rendering the homosexual visible is the necessary companion to the strategy of rendering homophobia – and other anti-homosexual mechanisms – equally visible. This is especially relevant for the study of sociocultural contexts where homosexuality is silenced or stigmatised, and of popular homophobic texts that dare to mention homosexuality – even if only to abhor it – and therefore to confer some sort of visibility on it.

Spanish "sexy comedy" and popular culture

PEDRO: ¡Están extraordinarias! ¡Y cómo les gusta el sol!

ANTÓN: ¡El sol, la naranja, y el hombre español como tú!

The position of popular genres in the late years of the Franco regime was exemplary of one of the most common topics relating to popular culture in general, namely that popular Spanish films were at once ideologically superficial, politically reactionary and commercially successful. Caparrós Lera describes the comedies of directors such as Pedro Lazaga, José María Forqué, Mariano Ozores, and Ramón Fernández as "cine chabacano, listo para ser consumido por el gran público", an ideologically exploitative form of film that masked its political conservatism behind a "fachada de pretendida liberación de tabúes" (Caparrós Lera 57–58). Popular genres were neatly differentiated from the more intellectually appealing films of Carlos Saura, and also from the so-called *tercera vía*. Frequently mentioned popular comedies include Pedro Lazaga's *No desearás la mujer de tu prójimo* (1968), *Vente a Alemania, Pepe* (1971), and *La ciudad no es para mí* (1965), Fernando Merino's *Préstame quince días* (1971), and *No desearás la mujer de tu vecino* (1971), José Luis Sáenz de Heredia's *Pero... ¡en qué país vivimos!* (1967), Manuel Summers's *No somos de piedra* (1968), José María Forqué's *El triangulito* (1970), Ramón Fernández's *No desearás al vecino del quinto* (1970), and Vicente Escrivá's *Lo verde empieza en los Pirineos* (1973). According to Torres, "Entre ellas destaca *No desearás al vecino del quinto* por ser la que tiene mayor éxito, convertirse en un fenómeno que lanza el subgénero y al actor Alfredo Landa, darse en ella sus principales características y tener un título que, con algunas variantes, se repite con frecuencia" (274–75). The genre epitomised by *No desearás al vecino del quinto*, attracted several different labels, most of which stressed either the centrality of soft-porn themes and techniques or the national Spanish market that conditioned the movies, or both.

A successful tourism campaign of the Franco years popularised the slogan "Spain is different". As critics and historians would later explain, that slogan encapsulated perhaps the most telling truism about Spain at the time. Everything was different in Spain, not only because of the idiosyncrasies of its peoples and traditions, but also because of the increasingly exceptional status of its political regime. One of the cinematic implications of this essential difference was the tightening of censorship in the late sixties and early seventies, precisely when most European countries were rapidly softening their censorship practices. This asymmetry partly explains several peculiarities of the film industry of the time, from the production of dual versions of the same film (one for domestic consumption, observing official censorial codes, and one for export, typically including female nudes), to the enormous popularity enjoyed by foreign actresses such as Ira von Furstemberg and *Nadiuska*. Torres uses the term *comedia a la española* as a national marker of difference in relation to the more open comedy of manners prevalent in other European countries:

> Hundiendo sus raíces en el sainete, de sólida raigambre madrileña, y en la comedia de parejas, importada de Italia una década antes, comienzan a hacerse comedias que giran en torno a la insatisfacción sexual del español medio. (Torres 274–75)

But perhaps the cleverest denomination is the one used by Vanaclocha: *Comedia Celtibérica*, referring to the primitive inhabitants of the Iberian Peninsula – Celts and Iberians – and therefore insinuating the retrograde libidinal deficiencies of what Jordan and Morgan call "the hugely inflated but constantly frustrated libido of the typical, repressed Iberian male, epitomised in the figures portrayed by Alfredo Landa" (Jordan and Morgan-Tamosunas 64–65; *cf.* Vanaclocha).

Another denomination for the genre, or at least for some of the films, was named after Alfredo Landa and his leading role in *No desearás al vecino del quinto*. "*Landismo*" was a popular but somewhat derogatory term for Spanish movies featuring the so-called average (male) Spaniard – a cheeky, smart-alec, sexually voracious but ultimately repressed middle-aged man (Torreiro 364). Juan José Alonso Millán, the scriptwriter of *No desearás al vecino del quinto*, was one of the main architects of the formula and wrote many of the scripts. Borau gives more credit to Alonso Millán for *landismo* than to Alfredo Landa himself.[10] In the case of *No desearás*, for instance, both Landa and Alonso Millán were more truly *landistas* than the director, Ramón Fernández – a commercial filmmaker with no auteurist inclinations who specialised in comedies.[11]

The genre was deeply homophobic, as was the rest of social and cultural life in Spain under the Franco regime. Homosexuality was an axiomatic perversion whose justification would be unimaginable. As a theme in novels or in films, it was simply banned by the Censorship Code of 9/2/1963,[12] whose article 8–4 declared: "Se prohibirá: la justificación del divorcio como institución, del adulterio, de las relaciones sexuales ilícitas, de la prostitución y, en general, de cuanto atente contra la institución matrimonial y contra la familia". And article 9: "Se prohibirá: la presentación de las perversiones sexuales como eje de la trama y aún con carácter secundario, a menos que en este último caso esté exigida por el desarrollo de la acción y ésta tenga una clara y predominante consecuencia final" (in Vanaclocha 253).

Anxieties, schizophrenia, panic

> DOCTOR: De momento el paciente sufre un fuerte trauma psíquico.
> JACINTA: Y eso del trauma ¿es grave?
> DOCTOR: No. Sólo requiere un poco de paciencia.

In his monumental reference sourcebook on Spanish homosexual culture, Alberto Mira denounces *No desearás al vecino del quinto* as "peor que homófoba", "oligofrénica, machista", and shows dismay at the fact that it is "todavía una de las películas más taquilleras en la historia del cine español" (Mira Nouselles 534). For Mira, the huge box-office success of the movie is proof that in Spain "nadie quiere hablar seriamente de la homosexualidad". There is, certainly, something deeply disturbing in the fact that the movie seems to be nearly as popular today as it was three decades ago, when homosexuality was still a crime and the Censorship Office had the prerogative to ban any film or novel featuring homosexual characters. It could be argued, however, that the film occupies in today's culture a different position from that which it occupied in the early seventies. Today's viewers are better equipped to perceive the satire and the caricature, but perhaps they have lost the competence to appreciate the anxieties that lie beneath its surface. If, following Mira, it is true that the film celebrates homophobia, naïvety and sexism, it is also true that Spanish society of the seventies – at least the segment of society that was allowed to speak up in the media – was proud of those "virtues". It was a society with no notion of what homophobia was,[13] and with an extraordinarily limited knowledge of what homosexuals looked like. It was, however, a society with an acute sensibility towards change – any kind of change – and particularly towards change in traditional morals, presumably as a powerful emblem of political changes or changes to lifestyle. Queer viewers might enjoy today the seemingly innocuous homosexual caricature of Alfredo Landa, but we should also be reminded that this caricature had a disproportionately subversive effect in 1970. *No desearás al vecino del quinto* exudes signs of distress provoked by the anxiety of narrating the homosexual without actually giving it a name. It is indeed a psychotic text that begins with the interdiction of desire (*"No desearás"*)[14] and progresses towards the denial of all forms of desire and of homosexual desire in particular. The homosexual taboo – the word is never uttered, and the censor asked that the word "mariquita" in the last scene be removed – is coupled with two sets of dualities so extreme in their consequences that one critic has referred to the movie as openly schizophrenic (see Carlos Losilla in Pérez Perucha 682).

The long-standing struggle between tradition and modernity is one of these schizophrenic dualities. This is, incidentally, a recurring topic in the Spanish "comedias desarrollistas" of the 50s and 60s, and it has been argued that it is one of the main focuses of contemporary Spanish culture. The movie starts with a conversation between a gynaecologist dressed in white and Jacinta – his fiancée. When the self-important doctor asks her to tell the "whole truth", he is using an old rhetorical device and their conversation becomes a modern version of the confession. The woman's explanation then gives the movie's thesis, and her voice off camera is coupled with documentary-style shots of Toledo:

De todo lo sucedido tiene la culpa la ciudad donde Pedro y yo hemos nacido y en la que hemos pasado toda nuestra vida. Porque hoy en día vivir en una capital de provincias es difícil, ¿sabe? Todo se complica, se vive pendiente de los demás. Hay una confusión tremenda de ideas, de gustos, de opiniones. El aire moderno contrasta con los viejos prejuicios. Las antiguas tradiciones se entremezclan con tendencias revolucionarias. En fin, somos demasiado provincianos para ser modernos y demasiado modernos para ser provincianos. Estamos acomplejados.

The rest of the movie conveys Jacinta's narrative of Pedro's relationship with the couturier Antón, their sexual adventures in Madrid, and their peculiar business arrangements – Pedro in his clinic and Antón in his salon. Although Jacinta's introduction attempts to establish a balance between tradition and modernity, traditional moral values and apprehensions about modern lifestyles are openly ridiculed throughout the movie. Pedro's mother, for instance, is portrayed as an extremely fainthearted woman who is afraid of change and who typically refuses to admit that her 30-year-old son is no longer a child. Jacinta's father is characterised as an intransigent, right-wing member of the bourgeoisie who looks with disdain on his daughter's fiancé of 12 years because gynaecology is not a decent enough profession. Social events attended by these families include cooking contests for the women, fancy dress parties "en pro de la juventud descarriada", and so on. Ultimately, though, it is tradition, and not modernity, that is sanctioned and endorsed by the narrative. Thus, after all the meanderings and sexual misunderstandings in the plot, the happy wedding of Pedro and Jacinta seeks to demonstrate that heterosexual marriage is a more practical and essentially superior form of human relations than one-night stands or, indeed, homosexuality. From this simultaneously moral and practical point of view, the confrontation between tradition and modernity adopts the form of a confrontation between safety and risk, which is explored through two well-known binaries. First, the topical opposition between the big city (Madrid) as an emblem of modernity and rural or provincial places (in this case, Toledo) as the space of tradition. The modernity of Madrid is illustrated positively by science and progress, as Pedro goes to Madrid to attend a conference on gynaecology, by cosmopolitanism, represented by European flags and foreign languages, and by its transformative influence – Pedro will return from his Madrid trip feeling different: "He cambiado, soy otro, hay un hombre nuevo en mí … un hombre feliz". But this is precisely the negative aspect of modernity: his mother's reply ("Me gustabas más antes") is paradigmatic of the traditionalist distrust of things modern. In addition, Madrid is the site of all moral perils epitomised by sexual promiscuity. The second binary is the opposition between the virtuous Spanish woman and the dubious and usually predatory foreigner. Pedro's stay in Madrid ends up being longer than expected because he casually meets Antón in a disco. Feeling trapped, Antón tells Pedro the truth about his sexuality and about the homosexual farce he is forced to maintain in order to keep his feminine clientele. Suddenly, Pedro gets excited with Antón's libidinal excess and he entirely forgets to go back to Toledo. Both men spend several days in Antón's apartment in Madrid. A neighbouring apartment is used by visiting female flight attendants who provide Pedro and Antón with enough opportunities to satisfy their appetites. Swedes one day, Italians the next, but never Spaniards. If foreign – European – women are so modern, Spanish women are "naturally" decent and will never have sex outside marriage.

As a response to the growing demand for sexually explicit movies, this film features homosexuality, wild parties, sexual needs and frustrations, doctors, adultery, voyeurism, and so on. However, all these topics were inimical to the institution of marriage and therefore likely to be censored. These two opposing forces result therefore in the movie's double strategy of fascination with and rejection of the modern, risky, urban, European image of sex.

> [E]s esta combinación de implicación y distanciamiento, de constante atracción y rechazo con respecto a lo que se considera innombrable (el sexo en todas sus facetas), lo que inscribe a la película en su personalísimo *status*, algo que ninguna otra comedia de la época logró igualar. (Losilla in Pérez Perucha 681–82)

One of the most notable achievements of the script is the echoing of Spain's schizophrenic approach to modernity through a homosexual double life. The movie's double ideological standards are visible in its critique of the old-fashioned, narrow-minded, provincial Spain, and in its final punishment of Antón, the couturier. While all the other characters and the audience had been induced to believe that Antón was first homosexual and then a rogue bachelor, he happens to be a married man with several children. His wife had agreed to the homosexual charade, but she was in the dark about Antón's visits to Madrid. When she finds out she reacts angrily and forces her husband to go back to the homosexual routine at the salon to keep the business running – but she appoints herself as Antón's secretary and public relations officer in order to keep him under strict surveillance. Losilla concludes that the success of the film is due to the combination of its "impresionante capacidad para la asimilación y el eclecticismo" and its ability to draw on all the traditional resources of Spanish comedy – he mentions *vodevil* and *sainete*, and the caricature of *Nuevo Cine Español* in the films by Manuel Summers:

> Al año siguiente Roberto Bodegas y Alfredo Matas inaugurarían la llamada 'tercera vía' con *Españolas en París* (1971) y, entonces, todo quedaría ya claro respecto al film dirigido por Ramón Fernández: a medio camino entre lo viejo y lo nuevo, entre la muerte de una cierta comedia a la española y el nacimiento de otra, *No desearás al vecino del quinto* no sólo había fascinado al público español por el atrevimiento de sus temas o su inofensiva comicidad, sino también por su condición de irresistible

cajón de sastre, casi la historia entera de la comedia española de las décadas anteriores alegremente embutida en apenas ochenta frenéticos minutos. (Losilla in Pérez Perucha 682)

The other duality is represented by the typically Spanish opposition of *ser* and *parecer*, "being" versus "looking", and the poetics of deception that is prevalent in Spanish comedy genres. Asymmetries between what things are and what they seem to be offer the opportunity for a critique both of sexual identity and of social hyprocrisy, as well as an exploration of the gaze.

With respect to identity, the movie constructs a very effective *trompe l'oeil* around the two false homosexuals. Antón is believed to be gay before both the audience and Pedro, to the exclusion of other characters, find out that he is not. For a while, Pedro's mother and fiancée think that Pedro is just having fun in Madrid, and they decide to go and find him to see what is going on. They find out about Antón's apartment and infer that Antón and Pedro must be sharing it. In that moment, Pedro is "contaminated" with Antón's homosexuality in the eyes of his fiancée and his mother: for them, both Pedro and Antón are a gay couple living in Madrid. But, of course, Pedro and Antón are actually two heterosexuals cruising for sex. Pedro's fiancée and mother consider the situation serious enough to be definitive; Pedro and Antón consider the situation inconsequential. Moreover, Antón reveals himself to be a truly postmodern character in his unashamed ability to change identities with the same ease and rapidity with which he puts on his wig. The movie makes good use of the stigmatised status of homosexuality to point out the importance of dominant cultural perceptions in Spanish life. When Pedro is believed to have turned gay, the first concern of his fiancée and mother is to keep it private, not to create a scandal.

The eminently visual duality of "being" versus "looking" is also explored through the gaze. It is not only the characters who are forced into situations where they must look at or spy on others, sometimes using optical devices such as the telescope Antón and Pedro use to check the stewardesses' apartment from their balcony. The spectator is also confronted with situations that appeal to her/his voyeurism. The first appearance of Antón, for instance, with his semiotic excess of gay signs, is a provocation for the spectator to see him and interpret him as gay, rendering him legible, understandable. In a similar manner, the spectator will see Pedro pretending to be pregnant and delivering a baby, wearing an apron and cooking in front of his fiancée, as well as seeing her jumping to conclusions that the spectator knows are wrong. The movie, perhaps unlike many others of the time, allows the gaze to be both masculine and feminine.

Performed homosexuality

MUJER 1: Por lo visto eran amigos desde hace seis años.

MUJER 2: Caray con el doctor. Con razón no me miraba el escote.

MUJER 1: Sabes lo que te digo, que ahora me gusta más. Me parece más perverso.

MUJER 3: Chica, qué morbosa eres.

MUJER 2: Para que critiques a nuestros maridos. Porque serán más feos y más calvos, pero hay una gran diferencia, ¿no?

MUJER 1: Pues no sé qué decirte. Hay que ser más europeas.

For all its playful and deceptive flirting with representations of male homosexuality, *No desearás al vecino del quinto* is nevertheless a movie without homosexuals, and in some sense it is a movie about the limits and limitations of heterosexuality. One of the things that the comic genre allows to be underlined is how a heterosexual, Pedro, might have to prove his heterosexuality. Pedro's staging of heterosexuality echoes Antón's performance of homosexuality; that the former is genuine and the latter is faked is, from this viewpoint, irrelevant. The point, as Judith Butler has theorised for gender, is that sexual identity must be constantly performed and that performance must be constantly seen by someone else in order to be effective. There might be no genuine homosexuals in the movie, but there are plenty of homosexual performances – whose symbolic value is equally powerful, as the censors, who asked that all appearances of the false homosexual be removed, knew.

Unlike Pedro's rather restrained performance of heterosexuality, Antón's performance is marked by redundancy and excess in order to ensure the necessary degree of visibility. Alfredo Landa's excessive imitation was deemed by his contemporaries as the main reason for the enormous popularity of this movie.

> *No desarás al vecino del quinto* debe su gran éxito de público al nada sutil guión del dramaturgo especializado en comedias Juan José Alonso Millán, pero sobre todo a la eficacia de la composición realizada por el popular Alfredo Landa del peluquero homosexual Antón con su perrita Fifí. (Torres 277)

Both the script and Alfredo Landa's acting are indeed excessive in their approach to homosexuality. But excess, in this case, works in contradictory directions: it is thanks to excessive performance that homosexuality is rendered visible, but it is also thanks to excessive performance that the queer is under constant surveillance and control. Excess renders the homosexual both visible and innocuous.

Antón's excessive performance affects both the semiotic density of his *mise-en-scène* and the object of his imitation. Curiously enough, he is not trying to imitate any stereotyped model of femininity. His effeminacy is a parody of the only model of male homosexuality in Franco's Spain. This model had been slowly refined through everyday language and oral jokes over the years, probably as a popular stereotyping of decadent homosexual types that were openly visible in the large cities during the twenties and early thirties. The repressive regime of general Franco tried very hard to reduce as much as possible the social visibility of those then considered as perverts and inverted. The immediate effect of this campaign of silence and invisibility was, of course, the crystallisation of a highly stylised stereotype of the male homosexual as an excessive effeminate, immediately recognisable by his clothes, gestures, the pitch of his voice, conversation lines, profession, and typical situations. This stereotype displaced all other possible representations of homosexuality to such an extent that in 1970, when Alfredo Landa was assigned the construction of the gay couturier for *No desearás al vecino del quinto*, it was his only option, albeit one that was quite overdetermined. But if an important part of the success of Landa's Antón is its fidelity to the model, the other is its parodic nature, and in this sense the censorial code that prohibited the representation of true homosexuals was indeed providential. The movie emphasised that an essential ingredient of the stereotyped effeminate was precisely its referential nature: the effeminate had never been a fixed identity, nor a natural entity; it was a quotation of an abstract model of effeminacy, a second degree representation. Censorial practices prevented the script from developing a more realistic representation of the homosexual; instead, scriptwriter Millán Alonso created a fake homosexual, a man who was forced to re-create homosexuality for his clients, thus evidencing the distance between model and impersonation that lies behind most displays of effeminacy.

The conservative agenda of the movie is completed with the desexualisation of the homosexual. The excessive visualisation of Antón's drag is never complemented by any kind of gay sexuality, nor by displays of affection, nor by gay friends or signs of a gay culture. This was an important part of the domestication of the effeminate stereotype: it was innocuous because it was not sexually active – or was not seen to be sexually active. Therefore homosexuality was presented as a rather solitary exercise of manners, and never a social sexuality. The effeminate was rarely understood to be a transvestite, though: rather than a fake or imperfect woman, he was an imperfect man deprived of all mannish attributes – including, notably, sexuality.

Heterosexuality provides the grounds for the observance of the traditional rule of comedy that stipulates marriage as the canonical "happy ending". This generic convention, of course, is perfectly appropriated by the ideologically reactionary "sexy comedy" in its docile implementation of the right-wing Catholic tenets on reproductive family values. Despite all its pretentions, the movie ends with the preservation of both couples in the form of marriage.

This does not mean, however, that heterosexuality is absolved of its sins. There is no exculpation of male supremacy, although there is not an explicit condemnation of female subjugation. But, more importantly, male heterosexuality is presented as predatory, competitive, and secretive, to the point of creating the abject Antón, a predatory heterosexual who unashamedly uses a homosexual mask to achieve his libidinous and financial goals.

Heterosexuality is problematised. Antón makes strategic use of the homosexual stereotype for two reasons: in terms of pleasure, he derives more open and frequent contact with women than most heterosexuals – even if the contact is merely visual; with regards to his business, he derives more profits than his heterosexual neighbour(s) and competitors. Furthermore, he seems to be fully integrated and accepted by his clients and friends, and he is seen as a happy man and a prosperous entrepreneur. Therefore, for Antón, homosexuality pays off, and, as we will be told, his heterosexuality was never affected by his deceptive practices. For the undisputedly heterosexual gynaecologist things are just upside down: after 12 years of what seems a rather dull sentimental relationship there are still no prospects of marriage (meaning sex) with his fiancée, and his clinical business does not prosper precisely because of his (hetero)sexual appeal. For him, heterosexuality doesn't pay off. One of the climactic moments of the movie consists, tellingly, in the narrative of his apparently failed heterosexuality.

Homosexuality acquires an unexpected relevance because of its power to expose the fragility of the heterosexist order. The very presence of the gay character in the provincial society of the film acts as a catalyst for changes both in the domestic and the social orders. The heterosexual order is indeed queered by the mere possibility that a respectable member of society (a doctor, even if a dubious, sexually-tainted doctor, a gynaecologist) might be or become homosexual.

A final note

It is tempting to question whether the vulgar and undignified treatment of homosexuality in the movie ultimately has a dignifying effect. Again, this Janus-like movie seems to offer two opposing answers, for while it set one of the stereotypes that would allow homosexuals some sort of visibility in the Spain of the 70s and 80s, it was also deeply insulting for many homosexuals. Nevertheless, as early as 1974, it was argued that this movie, far from being a fantastic product of the imagination, had indeed a notable testimonial, documentary value:

> Esta película marcará decisivamente el futuro camino del cine erótico español. No es una película aberrante. Es, por desgracia, una película testimonial. Aberrantes son las causas que la convierten en testimonial y en el mayor éxito comercial del cine español de todos los tiempos. (Vanaclocha 214)

We now know that lesbian and gay liberation groups that had been working in Spain immediately after the passing of the *Ley de Peligrosidad Social* were arguing exactly in the same direction: the problem was not homosexuality, but, according to Enríquez, a "sick" society that was unable to overcome its aberrant misconceptions about homosexuality.

Works cited

Aliaga, Juan Vicente "Caza de brujas, visibilidad y homofobia: el caso Arny y los medios en España." *Gay and Lesbian Writing in the Hispanic World / Literatura gay y lesbiana en el mundo hispano.* Ed. Alfredo M.artínez-Expósito. Special number of *Antípodas: Journal of Hispanic Studies* 11–12 (1999–2000): 5–14.

Aliaga, Juan Vicente and José Miguel G. Cortés. *Identidad y diferencia: sobre la cultura gay en España.* Barcelona: Editorial Gay y Lesbiana, 1997.

Borau, José Luis and Carlos F. Heredero. *Diccionario del cine español.* Madrid: Alianza Editorial, Sociedad General de Autores y Editores, Fundación Autor, Academia de las Artes y las Ciencias Cinematográficas de España, 1998.

Butler, Judith. *Gender Trouble: Feminism and the Subversion of Identity.* New York: Routledge, 1990.

Caparrós Lera, José María. *El cine español bajo el régimen de Franco, 1936–1975.* [Barcelona]: Publicacions i Edicions de la Universitat de Barcelona, 1983.

Cleminson, Richard. "Male Homosexuality in Contemporary Spain: Signposts for a Sociological Analysis." *New British Hispanisms.* Ed. Chris Perriam. Special number of *Paragraph* 22.1 (1999): 35–54.

Dynes, Wayne R. "Introduction to Gay Male Literature." *Gay and Lesbian Literature.* Ed. S. Malinowski. Detroit: St. James Press, 1994. xiii–xv.

Enríquez, José Ramón, ed. *El homosexual ante la sociedad enferma.* Barcelona, 1978.

Eslava Galán, Juan. *Coitus interruptus: la represión sexual y sus heroicos alivios en la España franquista.* Barcelona: Planeta, 1997.

Guasch, Òscar. *La sociedad rosa*, Barcelona: Anagrama, 1991.

Hennessy, Rosemary. "Queer Visibility and Commodity Culture." *Cultural Critique* 29 (1995): 31–76.

Jordan, Barry y Rikki Morgan-Tamosunas. *Contemporary Spanish Cinema.* Manchester; New York: Manchester UP, 1998.

Llamas, Ricardo. *Teoría torcida: prejuicios y discursos en torno a la homosexualidad.* Madrid: Siglo XXI, 1998.

Martínez-Expósito, Alfredo. *Los escribas furiosos: configuraciones homoeróticas en la narrativa española actual*, New Orleans: University Press of the South, 1998.

Mira Nouselles, Alberto. *Para entendernos: diccionario de cultura homosexual, gay y lésbica*, Barcelona: Ediciones de la Tempestad, 1999.

Mirabet i Mullol, Antoni. *Homosexualidad hoy: ¿aceptada o todavía condenada?* Barcelona: Herder, 1985.

Moix, Terenci. (s.d.) "Un manifiesto gay: *Diferente*." *La gran historia del cine.* Ed. Terenci Moix. Madrid: ABC/Blanco y Negro, 1959.

Monterde, José Enrique. *Veinte años de cine español (1973–1992): un cine bajo la paradoja.* Barcelona: Ediciones Paidós, 1993.

Parker, Andrew and Eve Kosofsky Sedgwick, eds. *Performativity and Performance.* New York: Routledge, 1995.

Pérez Perucha, Julio. *Antología crítica del cine español 1906–1995: flor en la sombra.*

Madrid: Cátedra, 1997.

Smith, Paul J. *Laws of Desire: Questions of Homosexuality in Spanish Writing and Film, 1960–1990*. Oxford: Claredon Press, 1992.

Soriano Gil, Manuel. *Homosexualidad y represión: iniciación al estudio de la homofobia*, Madrid: Zero, 1978.

Torreiro, Casimiro. "Del tardofranquismo a la democracia (1969–1982)." *Historia del cine español*. Eds. Román Gubern, et al. Madrid: Cátedra, 1995. 341–398.

Torres, Augusto M. *El cine español en 119 películas*. Madrid: Alianza, 1997.

Vanaclocha, José. "El cine sexy celtibérico." *Cine español, cine de subgéneros*. Eds. Juan M. Company, Vicente Vergara, Juan De Mata Moncho, José Vanaclocha. Valencia: Fernando Torres, 1974. 195–284.

Notes

[1] A previous version of this paper was presented to the Second Annual Conference of the European Cinema Research Forum, *Screening Identities* (University of Wales, January 2002). I wish to express my gratitude to Rob Stone and Joe Hardwick for their help and generous feedback.

[2] *No desearás al vecino del quinto / Due ragazzi da marciapiede* (1970), a Spanish-Italian coproduction (Atlántida Films, Fida Cinematografica) directed by Ramón *Tito* Fernández with script by Juan José Alonso Millán and Sandro Continenza. There are remarkable similarities between this film and Mario Mattoli's *Un turco napoletano* (1953); Sandro Continenza took part in both scripts.

[3] The climate of social unrest during this period should be taken into account in any study of the reasons behind the enormous success of home-made light comedies. In December 1970 there were meetings of opposition forces and massive demonstrations of support for the regime in the Plaza de Oriente, while the Proceso de Burgos against 16 ETA activists triggered a resounding international outcry. Between January 1969 and June 1971 the government declared a state of emergency.

[4] The film is still frequently shown on national TV with extraordinary audience figures that make it competitive with the best American blockbusters. (*Cf.* Torres 274–75).

[5] Official figures in late 2001. "[P]ese al habitual menosprecio crítico hacia ese subgénero [...] *No desearás al vecino del quinto, La ciudad no es para mí* y *Pero... ¡en qué país vivimos!* ocupaban la segunda, tercera y cuarta posición entre los films con mayor número de espectadores del cine español hasta finales de 1987" (Monterde).

[6] *Diferente* has been described as "uno de los más exactos estudios de una personalidad homosexual efectuada en el cine mundial de la época". En el film, "la personalidad del homosexual aparece a cada momento y estalla, con tintes de misoginia despótica, cuando expresa su rechazo del sexo femenino en una sonada escena con la mujer que le pretende. Es toda una declaración de principios llevada a cabo con conmovedor convencimiento por el protagonista, Alfredo Alaria" (Moix).

[7] The Committee tried, though: "En general se deberán cuidar rigurosamente los excesos de exhibicionismo y de intimidad erótica, así como la presentación del supuesto homosexual [...] A excepción de la primera vez en que aparece Alfredo Landa en el salón de belleza, se deberán suprimir todas las intervenciones como supuesto invertido y las voces finales de las niñas diciendo 'mariquita'". (Pérez Perucha 681) None of these points were suppressed from the final version, though. I have identified some modes of construction of gay characters in Spanish film elsewhere (Martínez Expósito).

[8] Carlos Losilla gives a precise account of the views of the Censorship Committee on

the three successive versions of the movie submitted for approval. The first version, under the title *Yo engaño sin daño*, was rejected by the Committee on the grounds of "carga excesiva de lascivia". Other proposed titles were *Es cosa de hombres* and *Ama a tu prójimo y verás*. The final version was approved despite what the Committee perceived to be a "clima erótico y lascivo que parece ser consustancial al autor". The Committee's report specifically asked that the following line be removed: "Pues sabes lo que te digo, que ahora me gusta más. Me parece más perverso" (Pérez Perucha 681).

[9] A few months after the release of the film, the infamous *Ley de Peligrosidad Social* classified homosexual acts as illegal. The criminalisation of homosexuality triggered a gay liberation movement in Barcelona, Madrid, and other major cities (Eslava Galán; Mirabet i Mullol; Smith).

[10] In films such as *Mi marido y sus complejos* (Luis María Delgado, 1968), *Una vez al año ser hippy no hace daño* (J. Aguirre, 1968), *El señorito y las seductoras* (R. Fernández, 1969), *Simón, contamos contigo* (R. Fernández, 1971), *No desearás la mujer del vecino* (F. Merino, 1971), *El reprimido* (M. Ozores, 1974) or *Mauricio, mon amour* (J. Bosch, 1976), (Borau, Heredero and Academia de las Artes y las Ciencias Cinematográficas de España, 52).

[11] Apart from the more or less evident conflict between tradition and modernity, his films follow the *costumbrismo sainetesco* where the comic effect is brought in by repetition and excess. Ramón Fernández has co-directed the successful TVE series *Cuéntame cómo pasó* (2001), a nostalgic retrospective of the late stage of Francoism.

[12] This was the first code of practice for the censorship of films in the Franco years. Together with a fairer treatment of Spanish films in relation to foreign products, the systematization of censorship had been one of the key demands of the 1955 *Conversaciones de Salamanca*. Under the *aperturista* leadership of Fraga Iribarne, José María García Escudero restructured the censorship office in 1963; his *Código de Censura* would be in force until 1975 and would be implemented with more or less flexibility according to the prevalent *aperturista* or *inmovilista* tendencies of the government.

[13] The term would not appear in English until 1972. In Spanish it would be introduced as early as 1978, but would become current only in the 90s (Guasch; Soriano Gil).

[14] The interdiction is common to other titles of the genre, such as *No desearás la mujer de tu prójimo* (1968), by Pedro Lazaga, and *No desearás la mujer de tu vecino* (1971), by Fernando Merino. In these titles, personal objects are deprived of the personal "a" when they refer to women; the personal "a" is preserved, however, for the male object of *No desearás al vecino del quinto*. This is an extraordinary case of male chauvinism.

Limpiaculos, cucarachas *and* marujas: *Pilar Pombo's* monólogos *and the Older Spanish Woman*[1]

Lilit Zekulin Thwaites

In memoriam Pilar Pombo [1953–1999].
Con agradecimiento por tu amistad y tu inapagable sentido del humor.

In a 1990 article on contemporary Spanish theatre, Patricia O'Connor argues that since the end of the Spanish Civil War there has been a distinct progression in the works of women playwrights from, firstly, conformity to patriarchal values through adaptation and imitation during the 1940s to 1970s, to, secondly, protest via revision and subversion during the 1970s and 80s, and finally, to challenge, from the 1980s onwards ("Women Playwrights"). These three stages represent a move from dependency to independence, as women "turn [...] to female experience as the source of an autonomous art [...] redefining and sexualising external and internal experience", and frequently presenting it through a female voice and from a female perspective (Showalter 36).[2]

The fact that it has taken Spanish women playwrights so long to project a voice of their own is a reflection both of a society imbued with patriarchal values, and of a theatrical world ruled by economic profit, in which, with few exceptions, women have been allowed only a very minor and restricted professional role.[3] Commentaries, round table discussions and interviews with playwrights, actors and others involved in the theatre have stressed these points repeatedly over the last few decades.[4] Nevertheless, since the 1980s, various studies have suggested that the voices of female dramatists in Spain are being heard – or at least read – in growing numbers, despite the aforementioned obstacles. Wendy-Llyn Zaza's first class doctoral dissertation is a case in point. It analyses "la reflexión dramática sobre [la figura femenina literaria e histórica] frente a su representación en la Historia canónica. Asimismo, enlaza mujer, historia y sociedad dentro de los marcos del franquismo, transición y democracia en contestación a la historia oficial" (275). Among the conclusions reached by Zaza, two are particularly relevant, namely that "[l]a dramaturgia femenina contemporánea española gira en torno a tres temas inextricablemente unidos: mujer, historia y sociedad" (275–80); and that the voices of many of the authors of that "dramaturgia femenina" are challenging patriarchal values and traditions. One such voice, prematurely silenced by cancer in 1999, is that of Pilar Pombo, one of the few female writers who, in the first decades of the post-Franco era, deliberately chose to focus on the sorts of women and female experiences rarely found in the spotlight. Women much like those whom Rosa Montero has described as "*marujas*": ordinary, everyday women of all ages (including the elderly) who struggle to make a living and/or simply to survive in a society that either ignores them, or views them as virtually useless and ignorant:

> esas mujeres tradicionales, poderosas hacedoras de lo imposible, que [...] han cuidado infatigablemente de todo el mundo, antes que ellas mismas. Titánicas heroínas de lo cotidiano, la vida de cada día es obra suya ... mujeres de hierro y cenizas. (Montero, "María Galiana" 9)

Pombo, born in Madrid in 1953, and a lifelong *madrileña*, was actively involved from a young age, and on many levels, in the world of theatre, and subsequently added work in radio, television and film to her CV.[5] Her contribution to Spanish women's dramaturgy is evident on three main fronts, each of which demonstrates her commitment to theatre written by women, and challenges patriarchy directly. As a founding member and one-time secretary of the short-lived Asociación de Dramaturgas Españolas (inaugurated in 1987), she helped to formulate and promote the Association's primary objectives:

> reivindicar, sin ningún tipo de tinturas ideológicas ni pancartas feministas, la actividad dramatúrgica femenina y, a través del teatro, contribuir a mejorar la situación de la mujer dentro del contexto social, cuyo sistema se obstina todavía en cerrarle determinados ámbitos de actuación. (Oliva 11)

As the editor and publisher of inexpensive collections of shorter works by women dramatists which she sold through La Avispa, Madrid's renowned specialist bookshop dedicated to theatre and film, she made women's dramaturgy more accessible to a wider public, and hence potentially better known.[6] And finally, as a playwright, author of at least five longer plays and six monologues, she revised female stereotypes and presented a distinctly female perspective and commentary on contemporary Spanish society.

In other words, as a dramatist, Pombo was committed to counteracting the patriarchal notion of female as object or "Other" that has been prevalent for so long in the dramatic (and other) arts. Her commitment had little to do with a desire to conform to a particular ideology or to woo a particular type of audience or critic. She was in fact quite scathing about the potentially negative impact of theories and "-isms" on – and of – theatre, both in the transmission and in the critical analysis of "theatrical" messages.[7] Rather, her commitment was a recognition of the urgent need to present and disseminate a distinctly female discourse with a woman-centred focus, and female characters who were more likely to be the subject than the object of the dramatic action and the "male" gaze.[8] The monologue, particularly when delivered by female characters with a marked tendency to the same forthrightness as Pombo, would prove to be an ideal and effective vehicle for achieving her many goals.[9]

The monologue is a "minimalist" form of theatre in that it usually involves only a single actor and limited theatrical "distractions" and trappings (props, stage settings, lighting, etc). It is readily "portable", can be staged virtually anywhere at low cost, and can also be presented easily on radio and television. Four of Pombo's monologues were in fact broadcast on Spanish national radio on a weekly basis in March 1990 (Pombo RNE 3) All these factors make this type of theatre, and its message, accessible to a wide and diverse audience, including those who might otherwise be excluded due to their level of education, literacy, economic and/or social circumstances.

The fact that there is usually only one character on stage in a monologue means that s/he speaks with an unmediated voice, "selects" the topics for discussion unimpeded by the views, authority or power of others, and automatically commands attention, at least in the first instance. If, as in the case of Pombo's monologues (with one exception), that character is female, that factor becomes crucial and potentially challenging for, as the sole character and voice, she is empowered to speak "directly" and subjectively from her personal perspective, without fear of interruption or dismissal, as frequently occurs in "real" life. The views and experiences that she presents are specifically female (or filtered through a female perspective), and her solitary presence on stage means that the audience is able to form an intimate and direct relationship with her, no matter what their own cultural perspective, and its attendant "baggage" or prejudices, might be. In other words, as Sue-Ellen Case puts it in *Feminism and Theatre*, she is the subject or "producer of symbolic expressions" directing the gaze, rather than the created object (or target and recipient) of the male gaze (and male "cultural encoding").[10] For the duration of her monologue, she is woman-as-subject whose physical presence, comments, experiences and perspective on society are undeniably centre stage – precisely where patriarchal society normally does not allow her to be; and exactly where Pilar Pombo wants her.

But who are the women whose voices Pombo brings to our attention, and why has she turned the spotlight on them? Pombo portrays several generations and a social cross-section of women in the monologues, and extends the range even further through the one-sided telephone conversations, "dialogues" with characters off-stage, and imagined conversations with friends, relatives, neighbours and boyfriends. The youngest is Sonia, aged 19, from a working class background, and a hairdresser in a "peluquería de barrio". Despite the hard knocks she and her family regularly experience, she is still relatively optimistic – or perhaps naïve? – about her planned future which would seem to be the traditional one of marriage (to her less streetwise and sensible boyfriend) and children.[11] The oldest is Remedios, a pensioner confronted by the hypocrisy and materialism of a consumer society that expects her to fulfill the traditional role and obligations of a grandmother (babysitter and *limpiaculos*) until she is no longer "useful", and then anticipates depositing her in an old folks' home. Her chosen form of rebellion and self-assertion is guaranteed to set the metaphorical cat among the pigeons, some of which have in fact contributed to the process which leads to the final act of rebellion.

As a group, these are primarily "women of modest means, [unpolished rhetoric] and powerless circumstances [...] unsung heroines" with faults and foibles, who find it difficult to escape from the social and cultural expectations of their class (O'Connor, "Solidarity" 577). Women similar to those found in Rosa Montero's *Te trataré como una reina* or in many of her short stories and opinion pieces; women like many of the characters portrayed in Pedro Almodóvar's 1984 Film *¿Qué he hecho yo para merecer esto?*; or the pensioner Rosa and her daughter María, in Benito Zambrano's 1999 award-winning film, *Solas*. Women, to return specifically to Pombo's creations, who can be generous with fellow-victims, male or female, and damning of those who inflict physical or mental suffering on others; but equally, women adept at blaming others for their situation rather than themselves. For Pombo's society is no radical feminist utopia where all women are "good" and all men are "bad" simply because of their gender. Her women can be as cruel and unkind as their male counterparts; and in a number of instances, it is the mothers of the women in these monologues who have ensured that the patriarchal values they grew up with and were subjected to, are upheld by their daughters, regardless of the consequences.

Pombo herself provides an apt metaphor for her "heroines" in a typically pointed stage direction in *Amalia*. Among the noises to be heard in many Spanish patios and homes is that of "un pajarillo enjaulado que canta alegremente sus miserias" (1). Like this small, imprisoned bird, at times knowingly, at times unwittingly, but at all times inevitably, Pombo's women feel "enjauladas" by their gender, social class and condition; and it is only by dint of persistence and insistence that a few of them will taste freedom. They have suffered setbacks at the hands of others, and also, on occasion, because they have lacked the courage of their own convictions, or feared the consequences of breaking the mould. At the same time, many have also suffered because of their convictions and their rebelliousness. Yet most of these powerless insignificant women possess an internal fortitude, a determination to survive, and a sense of humour that is astonishing given the obstacles that society has put in their path, and the lives that they lead. Even when they are angry or frustrated, and have an inkling as to the causes of their "imprisonment", they can still often see the funny or positive side of life, and enjoy it, even if only momentarily. If an opportunity to rebel, to revisit an event, to "talk" it out and thereby see it in a different light, or from another perspective, presents itself, they are inclined to seize that opportunity, and if possible, use it to progress to the next round or stage in their lives.

Two of Pombo's monologues, *Amalia* (1986) and *Remedios* (1987), will serve as illustrations of this, and of other points discussed above. Amalia is a former "artista de espectáculo" in her fifties, who is now a cleaning lady. Life has dealt her some heavy blows, but she will not give in, nor will she lose her sense of humour and fun. This monologue is unusual because there is in fact another person on the stage who reacts to what she is narrating: a young photographer, Jaime, who barely intervenes except to listen (almost by default, initially) to the story of her life, and who finds her attitude so captivating and beautiful that he feels moved to capture her on film, while commenting: "¿Sabe por qué es guapa?, porque le ríen los ojos" (15).[12]

While telling Jaime her life-story – the life of a pretty but not very talented showgirl –, she reveals her experiences of the unpleasant side of human nature, such as professional rivalry, the perils of growing old, particularly in that profession, the sexual harassment that she had to endure, the bullying, and the destructiveness of gossip and innuendo. She also reveals the impact on her of social expectations and traditions – looking after her sick mother, for example, which required her to give up her career and subsequently become a cleaning lady in order to survive – and expected patterns of behaviour, including passivity and shyness in young girls. At the same time, as her story unfolds, it becomes clear that she has often challenged many of these taboos and expectations, both out of compassion for her fellow-beings, male and female, and out of a sheer delight in life, a delight which she has never lost.

The language in this monologue is full of spark, the encounter with Jaime is presented humourously, the scene is lively and vigorous, and Amalia, like many of Pombo's characters, consistently gives as good as she gets. When she first encounters Jaime in the flat she has come to clean, she keeps him at bay with a broom while she rings the owner, Srta. Cristina, to find out who he is and why he is there:

> ¡Y cómo puñeta no me ha avisado!... ¡Ah! que me ha dejado una nota, y ¿en dónde?, si se puede saber... En la huevera... No, si me parece un sitio muy apropiado para anunciar estas cosas... Lo que yo pienso del asunto [of finding Jaime in Cristina's bedroom], ya se lo dejaré en una nota ... Sí, como siempre (con sorna) en la huevera... (3)

She reveals to Jaime her admiration for other people who, like her, refuse to be stereotyped, like the little nun in the convent where she cleans free of charge because the nuns are even worse off than she is: "no tienen un duro; son de ésas que recogen pobres y viejos" (4). The nun in question is so small that she is worried she will be mistaken for a cockroach and stepped on. When Amalia comments on her un-nunlike sense of humour, she replies "no soy monja, soy una cucaracha disfrazada", and goes on to explain that she picked the name hermana Angustias "para despistar" (4). Humour and an innate sense of justice help Amalia and others like her to overcome the difficulties and prejudices they encounter on a regular basis in the course of their day-to-day existence. There is, however, also an undertone of sadness and of missed opportunities in her monologue – a keen awareness that she is getting older (14), for example, or the no longer possible marriage to Matías, the misunderstood and mistreated former stagehand for the show in which she used to perform.

The mix of personal and social commentary, humour and criticism gives an edge and a sense of reality to this monologue, without which some of its characters might otherwise seem a little too Pollyanna-like to be convincing.

Remedios, the sixty plus character in the monologue of that name, shares Amalia's occasionally sharp tongue and disrespect for social conventions and hypocrisy. Through Remedios, Pombo delivers a stinging attack on the plight of an often-ignored group of marginalised people – the elderly, male and female alike. Again, she focuses on stereotypical attitudes that impose certain types of behaviour, and a society which takes advantage of, and cares little about, (elderly) people with minimal or no power, while highlighting the degree to which Spain has entered the age of consumerism and self-centredness.

A pensioner widow, Remedios was persuaded by her daughter and son-in-law to sell her apartment in the friendly neighbourhood where she had lived for many years, and move in with them, so that her daughter could go back to work after the birth of her second child. As long as Remedios was useful for wiping bottoms and childminding, she was tolerated by her daughter and "soso" son-in-law. Now, however, she suspects that they want to put her in a home because they consider her a useless "vieja chocha"; a future she decides she will not accept. Importantly, she has met another pensioner and widower, Esteban, who wisely (she feels) has not given in to family pressure to sell his apartment, and who refuses to get rid of his beret and shave his beard simply to kowtow to his newly-elevated bank manager son. Clearly, Remedios approves of his attitude to life, an attitude that has contributed to her own growing assertiveness and rebelliousness.

Initially angry over the fact that her daughter and family have once again phoned at the last minute on a Saturday afternoon to tell her that they will not be home for lunch, she convinces herself that under the circumstances, the time has come to tell them about Esteban, and about her wish to marry him. She then proceeds to imagine the ensuing conversation with various family members, in particular with her much more traditional and conservative daughter, in the process revealing many of the problems that Spanish society has not yet tackled in relation to its older inhabitants. Humourously, ironically, sarcastically, angrily and at times sadly, she "explains" to her horrified daughter, Rosa, how she and Esteban met and became friends:

> ¡En un burdel! cada día estás más tonta, hija... ¡¡En el parque!! ¿Adónde
> pueden ir los viejos a nuestra edad y con la pensión que nos dan?... ¡Pues al
> parque, al parque a echar de comer a las palomas! que para eso creó Dios
> a las palomas... porque Dios, que es muy listo y para eso es Dios, se temió
> lo de las pensiones, y ... nos buscó una distracción baratita para que ni
> hiciéramos gasto, y nos llegara la pensión a fin de mes... (10)

Remedios makes clear to her daughter (while at the same time strengthening her own resolve) that she and Esteban need each other, they can help each other and feel useful, and be happy, but as she speaks, it becomes clear that there is much more to their being together than this: "ha sido muchos años de sentir un vacío en el cuerpo ... no sólo un hombre es importante ... *Lo importante es sentirse querido, útil, necesario* ..." (13. My emphasis). An old folks' home is not the answer, nor is remaining in a household where she is made to feel "un trasto viejo" (8).[13] As she reacts to the comments that she imagines her daughter would make, Remedios convinces herself that she does not need the family's permission either to leave, or to get married and that, in point of fact, she can even do without the priest's blessing. With that, she picks up the phone, calls Esteban, and tells him that she's coming over – for good! She leaves the family apartment, buoyed by the thought that her granddaughter will support her – "¡Jo, abuela, qué marcha llevas, es que alucinas!" (11) – chuckling at the difficulties her daughter will have in explaining her mother's sudden disappearance to the inquisitive neighbours, and looking forward to a night out at the movies with Esteban "como dos novios" (15).

In this monologue Pombo raises a number of rarely discussed social issues while showing how times are changing in Catholic and traditional Spain – issues such as loneliness and isolation, economic difficulties and dependency, mental and physical ill health, a lack of adequate resources, accommodation and activities for the elderly. She is not the first to have commented on these matters (e.g. Rosa Montero), and she is certainly not the last; and in Spain, just as in many other (developed) countries, the plight and situation of the elderly is a topic which continues to make headlines and plague those government bodies responsible for its resolution.[14] As Pombo suggests, pensioners need a life and companionship too; they still have much to offer society; they do fall in love and, incredible as it might seem to the scandalised Rosas of this world, there may even be sex after sixty, even if there are few places where it can be enjoyed by an old unmarried couple!

Pilar Pombo's monologues bring to life a group of women who are rarely found centre stage revealing their thoughts, fears, dreams, hopes, disappointments and pain to a group of strangers. Ordinary women similar to those described as *marujas* by Rosa Montero at the start of this article who have tirelessly put everyone else before themselves. Many of these women have never been inside a theatre, and could not imagine that their lives would be of interest to anyone. And it certainly would not occur to them as they stand centre stage and present Pombo's monologues that they, like their creator, could be a "nueva presencia femenina pionera de 'otra' voz y cultura, [que] rechaza la imagen establecida, juzgándola deformada y falsificada por intereses ajenos" (O'Connor, "El monólogo" 91). Pilar Pombo, like her characters, represents a breath of fresh air, humour and a fighting spirit within Spanish (theatrical) society; a voice which will be sadly missed.

Works Cited

Case, Sue-Ellen. *Feminism and Theatre*. London: Macmillan, 1988.

Cazorla, Hazel. "Conversación con Pilar Pombo." *Estreno* 25.2 (1999): 9–11.

"Conversación con el teatro alternativo." *Primer Acto* 248 (1993): 15–26

Doll, Eileen J. "El teatro madrileño de los 90: una encuesta." *Estreno* 25.2 (1999): 12–19, 47.

Flaquer, Lluís y Joan Soler. "La soledad en la sociedad urbana." *Barcelona, metròpolis mediterrània* 6 (1987): 141–46.

Gala, Antonio. *Anillos para una dama*. Madrid: Ediciones Jucar, 1974.

Gascón Vera, Elena. "From Struggle to Commitment: the Essays of Rosa Montero." *Spanish Women Writers and the Essay*. Eds. Kathleen Glenn and M. Mazquiarán de Rodríguez. Columbia, Miss: Univ of Missouri Press, 1998, 250–63.

Halsey, Martha and Phyllis Zatlin, eds. *Entre Actos: diálogos sobre teatro español entre siglos*. Pennsylvania: Estreno, Studies in Contemporary Theater 2, 1999.

Johnson, Anita. "Dramaturgas españolas: presencia y condición en la escena española contemporánea." *Estreno* 19.1 (1993): 17–20.

Monleón, José. "El teatro español que viene. Coloquio." *Primer Acto* 249 (1993): 32–48.

Montero, Rosa. *Crónica del desamor*. Madrid: Debate, 1979.

——. *Te trataré como a una reina*. Barcelona: Seix Barral, S.A., 1983.

——. "María Galiana. La vida empieza hoy" *EP[S]. El País Semanal*. 20 de febrero de 2000: 8–14.

O'Connor, Patricia. "Quiénes son las dramaturgas españolas contemporáneas, y qué han escrito?" *Estreno* 10.2 (1984): 9–12.

——. *Dramaturgas españolas de hoy: una introducción*. Madrid: Editorial Fundamentos, 1988.

——. "Solidarity and Re-Vision in the Plays of Two Spanish 'dramaturgas': Maribel Lázaro and Pilar Pombo." *Revista Canadiense de Estudios Hispánicos* 14.3 (1990): 573–78.

——. "Women Playwrights in Contemporary Spain and the Male-Dominated Canon." *Signs* 15 (1990): 376–90.

——. "El monólogo y la mujer: una minimeditación." *Art Teatral* 3.3 (1991): 91–92.

——. "Mujeres de aquí y allí." In Halsey and Zatlin: 158–69.

Oliva, María Victoria. "Las dramaturgas se asocian." *El público* 43 (1988): 41.

Ortiz, Lourdes, moderadora. "Nuevas autoras." *Primer Acto* 220 (1987): 10–21.

Pedrero, Paloma. "Algunas autoras de hoy y sus obras." *Primer Acto* 248 (1993): 56–57.

Pombo, Pilar. *Amalia*. Madrid: Monólogos, 1986.

——. *Una comedia de encargo*. 1986. [Typed copy from author].

——. *Isabel*. Madrid: Monólogos, 1987.

——. *Purificación*. Madrid: Monólogos, 1987.

——. *Remedios*. Madrid: Monólogos, 1987.

——. "*Remedios*: a Play by Pilar Pombo." Trans. Susan Jones. *Studies in the Humanities* 17.2 (1990): 179–90.

——. *Sonia*. Madrid: Monólogos: 1988.

——. *Ginés "El figurante"*. Madrid: Monólogos, 1990

——. *Remedios, Sonia, Isabel, Amalia*. RNE 3, Madrid. 4, 11, 18, 25 de marzo de 1990.

——. Personal interview. 22 Sept. 1994.

——. Letters to the author. 30 May, 28 June 1994, 20 Feb. 1999.

"¿Por qué no estrenan las mujeres en España?" *Estreno* 10.2 (1984): 13–25.
Ragué, María-José. "La mujer como autora en el teatro español contemporáneo." *Estreno* 19.1 (1993): 13–16.
Serrano, Virtudes. "El presente doloroso y esperanzado en la obra dramática de Pilar Pombo." *Estreno* 24.1 (1998): 39–43.
Showalter, Elaine. "Towards a Feminist Poetics." *Women Writing and Writing about Women*. Ed. Mary Jacobus. London: Croom Helm, 1979. 22–40.
Solas. Dir. Benito Zambrano. Maestranza Films, 1999.
Solé, Eulàlia, "Abuelas descuajaringadas." *La Vanguardia*. 4 de octubre de 2002: 23.
Yudin, Mary F. "'Nunca he tenido tiempo para ser ... yo': a Study of the Protagonists in Two Melodramas by Pilar Pombo." *Estreno* 21.1 (1995): 24–27.
Zaza, Wendy-Llyn. "Mujer, historia y sociedad: la dramaturgia femenina de la España contemporánea." Diss., The University of Auckland, 2000.

Notes

[1] I use the English word "monologue" throughout this article in the sense of "single actor play", to reflect this meaning of the Spanish *monólogo*. Mary Yudin, in her 1995 study of two of Pombo's *monólogos*, prefers the term "monodrama" for this type of play: "Although theater criticism in Spain uses the term *monólogo*, English criticism makes a distinction between a monologue: a speech that represents when someone would speak aloud in a situation with listeners, although they do not speak; dramatic monologue: a poem by a single character that reveals the character's thoughts; and monodrama: a theatrical presentation that features only one actor" (27).
[2] O'Connor adopts Adrienne Rich's term "re-vision, or 'seeing with fresh eyes'" to describe this final stage of development ("Solidarity" esp. 573–74).
[3] Ana Diosdado is an obvious if somewhat controversial exception. Critics such as Lázaro Carreter, Zatlin and O'Connor are uncertain about the strength of her commitment to writing plays that challenge patriarchal attitudes and conventions. As O'Connor puts it, there is at best an "ambivalent tone [... that] informs much of Diosdado's theatre" ("Women Playwrights" 379–85). See also O'Connor's later article, "Mujeres de aquí y de allí".
[4] See, for example, Ortiz, O'Connor ("¿Quiénes"), Monleón, Ragué and Johnson, as well as "¿Por qué no estrenan las mujeres en España?" and "Conversación con el teatro alternativo". Pilar Pombo's *Una comedia de encargo* and her monologue *Ginés "el figurante"* dramatically portray this reality. For a more recent commentary on the theatre scene in Madrid see Doll's 1999 survey.
[5] Hazel Cazorla's 1998 conversation with Pombo not only provides biographical details, but enables the reader to "hear" Pombo's views directly, and gain an insight into her personality. The articles by Serrano and Yudin, and Susan Jones's introduction to her translation of Pombo's *Remedios* also contain biographical information.
[6] *Cuadernitos de Mari Pili* and *Monólogos* are two such collections which Pombo produced on a home computer and sold as inexpensively as possible through La Avispa. Her aim was to make women's theatre more readily available, and its views more widely disseminated (Pombo, "Personal Interview").
[7] Pombo believed that any attempt to highlight theory must not be carried out at the expense of the text. She felt that strident feminism is often prepared to sacrifice text to theory: "Siempre he estado en contra de ese feminismo radical y estridente [...] una empieza a estar un poco harta de todas esas feministas, aunque yo diría más bien

'hembristas', que tratan de ver por todos los medios 'el símbolo opresor del falo'" ("Letters").

[8] "Gaze" in the sense of: "[t]he way the viewer perceives the woman on stage" (Case 118). Case is adapting to theatre E. Ann Kaplan's (psychosemiotic) "concept of the male gaze [which] asserts that representations of women are perceived as they are seen by men [... where] 'men' represent the male subject in capitalist patriarchy" (qtd. in Case 118).

[9] In the introduction to her article on Rosa Montero's essays, Gascón Vera refers to Theodor Adorno's definition of the essay and his view that "the essayist is always questioning reality, exploring it to its very limits, and, thus, overturning what is considered canonical and accepted by the community" (250). One can readily argue that Pombo is striving for these same goals with her monologues, thus extending Gascón Vera's comment that Adorno's "definition of the essay brings it close, theoretically and a priori, to other kinds of literary activity, such as poetry or poetic prose" (250–51).

[10] Clearly, a majority of the audience will be directing a "male gaze" at her; but what they see and hear will be unmediated/uninterpreted by male writers, actors and potentially, directors. Again, I borrow from Sue-Ellen Case, Chapter 7.

[11] I have deliberately chosen to use colloquial language and expressions in those sections of the article where I discuss the monologues in an attempt to reproduce the language of the women themselves. Again, it is worth emphasising that Pombo is one of the few women dramatists who focus on the largely un(der)represented female lower and working classes, and consistently uses the colloquial language and idioms of these groups where appropriate. Rosa Montero would be a good example of a prose writer who demonstrates a similar principle in some of her works, e.g. *Crónica del desamor*.

[12] This is one of the few times that Jaime expresses himself vocally, as he has a cold, and has conveniently (and perhaps ironically) lost his voice. His camera and the photos he takes – his gaze – serve as a substitute for his voice and opinions.

[13] Jimena, the Cid's widow, expresses similar sentiments in Antonio Gala's 1974 play *Anillos para una dama*: "De lo que tengo gana es de que se me quiera ... un cariño a mi lado al que le tenga que decir: Basta, Minaya. No me mires así: está toda la casa por hacer" (95). The two older protagonists (male and female) of *Solas* also stress the importance of friendship and company, of helping each other, of being useful and of not admitting defeat – thereby also staying young at heart: "no voy a vivir como los viejos"; "uno no está derrotado cuando le vence el enemigo sino cuando admite la derrota".

[14] See, for example, Flaquer and Soler (1987) or a recent opinion piece by Eulàlia Solé in *La Vanguardia* on "las abuelas explotadas", a response in part to two earlier articles in that newspaper's weekend "Magazine".

Catalonia and the Postcolonial Condition

Stewart King

This article explores postcolonial approaches as a means of interpreting literary production from Catalonia. Given that it is one of the wealthiest and most industrialised regions in Spain – a country with a long and not necessarily proud history of colonisation – such an approach may appear to confirm some critics' reservations about the inappropriate proliferation of postcolonial studies. That is to say, they see postcolonialism as functioning as a "roving thematic, easily affixed to almost any number of locations" (Murray and Riach 9). While acknowledging and responding to such reservations, this article seeks to show how the Spanish State has sought to colonise Catalonia by attempting to suppress its culture and identity through the imposition of an homogeneous "Spanishness". It examines ways in which several Catalan writers engage with and contest the discourses of Spanishness. Rather than seeing postcolonialism as a template which can be neatly fitted to the Catalan situation, my discussion will conclude by exploring the limits of current Catalan postcolonial studies in analysing the emergence of new Catalan identities.

At its most basic definition, postcolonialism is "the study of the ideological and cultural impact of Western colonialism and in particular of its aftermath – whether as a continuing influence (neocolonialism) or in the emergence of newly articulated independent national and individual identities" (Brooker 170). As Brooker suggests, the aim of Western colonialism was not simply the control of territories and resources by a foreign power; it also sought to colonise cultural spaces through a discourse which justified and legitimised their control of particular territories.

The question of representation, particularly self-representations, is at the heart of colonial discourses and postcolonial resistance. For Edward Said, "stories are at the heart of what explorers and novelists say about strange regions of the world" (Said xiii). The European colonisers claimed lands, justified their superiority and made sense of their overseas possessions through a variety of written texts, from legal documents, historical and anthropological studies, travellers' tales and letters, to more traditional literary texts, such as novels and poems. According to Said, "[t]he power to narrate, or to block other narratives from forming and emerging, is very important to culture and imperialism, and constitutes one of the main connections between them". Similarly, stories were employed by colonised peoples "to assert their own identity and the existence of their own history" in opposition to imperial representations of them (Said xiii). This focus on narrative is not to suggest that colonialism and anti-colonial resistance was little more than a textual exercise. Between the lines of such narratives can be read struggles for the control of geographic and social spaces.

Colonisation

An understanding of the historical, geographical and cultural specifics of the colonised and of the colonising power is central to any postcolonial approach. To date, several critics have used postcolonial theories to interpret literature from Catalonia (Boada, "Nationalism"; Boada, "Nacionalisme"; Palau Vergés; King, "Orquestando"; Crameri 117–120). Despite their readings of Catalan literature from a postcolonial perspective, none of these critics, with the exception of Crameri, goes any way towards developing satisfactorily an explanation of why and how Catalonia can be interpreted within a postcolonial framework.

In two studies on short stories written by Irish and Catalan women writers, Irene Boada sees many cultural and political similarities between Ireland and Catalonia. She argues that postcolonialism is a valid interpretative tool because these two European nations are considered bilingual societies, both are in the shadow of cultural and political giants, both respond to their subordinate position in political and literary terms as ex-colonial societies, both of them experienced a period of cultural renaissance in the nineteenth century, and finally both have a similar degree of self-questioning, in particular, what it means to be Catalan or Irish (Boada, "Nationalism" 9). Despite her insightful readings of Catalan women's writing, Boada unfortunately takes it for granted that Catalonia has been colonised and does not address just how this cultural and linguistic colonisation has occurred. Unlike Boada, in another study of Catalan women writers and national concerns, Palau Vergés makes brief reference to attempts by the Franco regime to impose upon Catalonia, the Basque Country and Galicia an homogeneous Spanishness based on a mix of Castilian and Andalusian culture (173). Like Palau, my own earlier contribution to Catalan postcolonial studies also limited itself to the ways in which Catalan literature can be seen to resist the cultural practices of the Franco regime.

In contrast to previous postcolonial approaches, Kathryn Crameri sees the "Spanish" colonisation of Catalonia as a phenomenon which precedes Francoism by several centuries. She argues that the colonisation of Catalonia was very different to that experienced by indigenous Latin Americans, as there was no violent beginning, but rather a series of intermixing of peoples and cultures from the fifteenth century onwards (118). This intermixing may be interpreted as nothing more than the process of nation-building. Such an interpretation, however, does not take into account the political and cultural struggles between different regions which have resulted in the formation of the Spanish State as we know it today. In order to understand better this process, it is necessary to explore the concept of internal colonisation.

Drawing on Gramsci's notion of internal colonisation, Michael Hechter argues that national development is predicated upon a core region which dominates peripheral regions politically and exploits them materially (9). Internal colonisation occurs when core regions with cultural practices distinct from those of the periphery – such as southeast England, L'Ille de France, and Castile – impose them upon the periphery as if it were a foreign colony (Hechter 25–33; McClintock 257). The historian Peter McPhee provides a relevant example of this in his article "A Case-Study of Internal Colonization: The *Francisation* of Northern Catalonia". McPhee argues that "a myth or ideology of national unity has been developed to explain, justify, and maintain the existing territorial order" of metropolitan France (399). In the case of Northern Catalonia, this myth deliberately obscures a long history of legal, political and cultural measures designed to denigrate Catalan culture as "second-class", "regional", or "premodern". McPhee cites laws promoting the French language and the banning of Catalan in education and administration. The effectiveness of these laws, and the attitudes which underpinned them, were further enhanced by the emigration of Catalans to other parts of France for economic reasons, as well as the immigration of French-speaking holiday makers and retirees into Northern Catalonia. The myth of French cultural and linguistic superiority led many Catalans to accept that it was necessary to abandon their Catalanness and become simply French in order to participate and share in the benefits of the French nation.

McPhee's analysis of the processes of internal colonisation is directly relevant to the political, social and cultural context south of the Pyrenees, where a similar, if less successful, attempt at internal colonisation also took place. While Catalonia was joined dynastically with Castile in 1478 with the marriage of the Catholic Monarchs, their union and the subsequent fall of Granada in 1492 did not result in the creation of a united Spain as some conservative historians have claimed (Barton 120). Instead, both realms maintained different political, administrative and legal systems. Furthermore, the various attempts at centralisation resulted in out-right conflict, such as the Reapers' War of 1640–1652, the War of Spanish Succession of 1701–1714, and more recently the Spanish Civil War of 1936–1939.

The implementation of political and cultural centralism in Catalonia followed the War of Spanish Succession. Upon winning the war, Philip V set out, by right of military conquest (Benet 14), to follow the centralist model of his grandfather, Louis XIV, and restructure the different political and legal systems within his realm. In Catalonia, the new legal code – the

Decreto de Nueva Planta – meant the imposition of laws that suppressed Catalan political and legal institutions and reinforced Castilian hegemony. For example, the Castilian legal system was given primacy over the Catalan one. Castilian was made the mandatory language for all government correspondance. Autochthonous institutions, such as the *Generalitat*, the *Diputació* and Barcelona town council were abolished and replaced with a "foreign" institution – the *Real Audencia del Principado de Cataluña*. The universities of Barcelona and Lleida were also closed and reformed into a single university and relocated to the rural town of Cervera, which had been loyal to Philip. According to British historian, J. H. Elliott, this brought about a fundamental political and cultural shift as "Philip V, unlike Philip IV, was not merely King of Castile and Count of Barcelona; he was also King of Spain" (377).

The *Decreto de Nueva Planta* was only the first large scale attempt at Castilian dominance. From the eighteenth century onwards, successive laws were regularly passed which banned the use of Catalan or limited its use in favour of Castilian. These included prohibiting Catalan in schools (1768 and 1857) and the obligatory teaching of Castilian (1834, 1838, 1849, 1870). Plays written in languages other than Castilian were not allowed to be performed according to statutes in 1801 and 1867. A series of bills were passed through parliament making Castilian the only legally acceptable language for accounting in 1772, for legal transactions in 1862, for entries in the Civil Registry in 1870, and in the Property Registry in 1915. Even teaching the catechism exlusively in Castilian was made law in 1902.[1]

Such legislation and the dominance of Castilian-language culture within the Spanish State quickly transformed Catalan culture. The Catalan language was even dismissed by some highly influential eighteenth-century proto-Catalanists, such as Antoni de Capmany and Antoni Puigblanc, as belonging to a bygone era (Jorba 129). It was even seen to hinder national (read Spanish) development and to deny Catalans full participation in state affairs. The abovementioned laws and attitudes provoked a cultural crisis in Catalonia by the mid-nineteenth century. In 1857, in an article titled simply "Cataluña", Joan Mañé i Flaquer argued that the centralising project had come at a terrible cost to Catalonia as "el catalán ha dejado de ser catalán, sin ser por esto más español" (430).

This crisis was the source of Catalonia's nineteenth-century cultural and literary revival known as the *Renaixença*. Whilst it is important to recognise that the *Renaixença* was not a unified movement and that many aspects of its cultural and linguistic agenda were contested, it aimed broadly to recover a Catalan identity which was seen as being marginalised by a foreign "Spanish" culture. As such, this movement can be read as an early attempt at cultural decolonisation. An analysis of the *Renaixença* as a process of decolonisation and national reconstruction is beyond the scope of the present article. Suffice to say that from its tentative steps in the nineteenth century, Catalan cultural nationalism developed and matured at the turn of the century with the *modernista* and *noucentista* cultural movements, and came to enjoy electoral success with the *Mancommunitat* (1914–1925) and with the restoration of the *Generalitat* in 1932.

This development was severely curtailed by the victory of the "Nationalist" forces in the Spanish Civil War. It has been argued that the Civil War was as much a struggle over different conceptions of Spain and Spanishness as it was over issues of democracy and fascism, social justice, and so forth (Boyd: 86). Franco's victory resulted in the imposition of an understanding of national identity as conceived by the dictator. At the heart of this conception of Spain was a discourse of Spanishness which saw the country's cultural and political unity based on Castilian language and culture:

> España se organiza en un amplio concepto totalitario, por medio de instituciones nacionales que aseguren su totalidad, su unidad y continuidad. El carácter de cada región será respetado, pero sin perjuicio para la unidad nacional, que la queremos absoluta, con una sola lengua, el castellano, y una sola personalidad, la española. (Franco Bahamonde 226)

The British hispanist, Paul Preston, argues that Franco's attitudes towards governing were fundamentally colonialist. They were shaped by his experience in Spain's colonial war in Morocco and then transposed to the Spanish arena. According to Preston, Franco saw "the colonised [as] children who needed a firm paternal hand". In a peninsular context, vociferous condemnation of the Moroccan wars by leftists and Catalan nationalists, led Franco to consider them "to be as dire an enemy as rebellious tribesmen" and hence, that the "rebellious" Spaniards, just like the Rif tribes, had to be repressed and governed harshly (Preston 49). This attitude was clearly manifested in the supression of the Asturian miners' uprising in 1934 and the treatment meted out to those he considered to be *antiEspaña* several years later during the Civil War and immediately afterwards.

For Franco, the limited independence given to Catalonia and the Basque Country during the Second Republic threatened the very existence of Spain and he even claimed that it was the main reason for his decision to rebel against the Republican government. This led to the most thorough attempt at internal colonisation not only in Catalonia, the Basque Country and Galicia, but throughout the entire country.

In line with his Castilian centralism, Franco sought to eradicate firstly, and later marginalise, those cultures which did not conform to his vision for the "new" Spain. In its desire to suppress future Catalanist sentiments, the regime sought to prohibit many aspects of Catalan culture, particularly the language. Measures taken by the regime included banning Catalan as a subject and language of instruction in schools and universities. Hundreds of thousands of books written in Catalan were thrown on bonfires or pulped

(Conversi 111). Catalan was completely excluded from the mass media in the earlier years of the regime, and later was only allowed at times of low viewing, such as the middle of the night. In an attempt "to establish at least partial control over reality, geography, history and subjectivity", baptismal and place names were Castilianised and monuments to famous Catalans were either destroyed or, like the statue to Casanova, were put into storage where they were eventually found and returned to their original standing place with the coming of democracy (Gilbert and Tompkins 165).

Just as the regime attempted to block alternative formulations of national identities from emerging, it also sought to impose its own interpretation – narrative – of what constituted Spanishness upon the nation. The regime attempted this by the imposition of a hegemonic view of history which emphasised cultural and territorial unity, and by promoting Castilian-language culture in Catalonia, the Basque Country and Galicia (Samsó 23; King, "Transformando" 26–27).

Franco's influence on the cultural life of Catalonia was far more extensive than that enjoyed by previous centralist rulers. Whereas in the past, Castilianisation had affected primarily the Catalan middle- and upper-classes, the regime was able to enter almost every household via its control of the mass media, which included – after 1956 – the new medium of television. The regime used these media to articulate its vision of the state and to silence alternative national discourses. This hegemony was further strengthened by the regime's control of mass education which was used to inculcate children in the conservative principals of the regime.

Despite this extensive influence, shortly after Franco's death in 1975 the vision of Spain for which he had fought at such great cost was progressively dismantled as Spaniards embraced democracy, free speech and cultural diversity. With respect to the "historic nationalities", the 1978 Constitution granted limited autonomy to Catalonia, the Basque Country and Galicia as well as co-officiality to Spain's non-Castilian languages in those regions where they are spoken. In Catalonia, political autonomy has resulted in the strengthening of Catalan culture and language in ways that can be clearly interpreted as an attempt at decolonisation. Yet unlike most postcolonial countries, Catalonia has not obtained its independence and it is still locked into a political relationship with the rest of Spain, with which many Catalans continue to identify.

Resistance

As can be seen in the brief analysis above, the Spanish State sought at different times to control cultural relations within its borders via repressive laws, violence and through the imposition of a discourse of Spanishness which marginalised non-Castilian-language cultures. Given that empire is as much about controlling cultures, histories and representations as it is about possessing territories and wealth, postcolonial societies have sought to challenge the assumptions of the colonial centre and to articulate new ways of expressing the identities of once-colonised peoples. Literature, in particular, is seen as playing an important role in the processes of decolonisation. According to Ashcroft et al., postcolonial literatures "emerged in their present form out of the experience of colonization and asserted themselves by foregrounding the tension with the imperial power, and by emphasizing their differences from the assumptions of the imperial centre" (2). Such literatures represent the lives, experiences and histories of those marginalised by imperial representations. A detailed analysis of literary responses to Catalonia's subordinate position within the Spanish State is beyond the scope of the present article. Instead, I wish to examine in this section three literary representations which seek to resist Castilian cultural hegemony via the articulation of a Catalan point of view. These are Joaquim Rubió i Ors's 1841 prologue to his collection of poems, *Lo gaiter de Llobregat*, Montserrat Roig's *El temps de les cireres* (1977), and Terenci Moix's *El dia que va morir Marilyn* (1969, rev. 1995).

The first large body of literary texts which self-consciously set out to articulate a Catalan point of view vis-à-vis the rest of the Spanish State appeared in the nineteenth century. This body of literature formed what is known as the *Renaixença*, or rebirth of Catalan culture. In what is considered the first *renaixentista* manifesto, the poet Joaquim Rubió i Ors affirmed:

> Catalunya pot aspirar encara á la independencia, no á la política [...]; pero si á la lliteraria, fins á la qual no se estent ni pot estendrer la política del equilibri. Catalunya fou per espay de dos seggles la mestra en lletras dels demés pobles; ¿perque puix no pot deixar de fer lo humillant paper de deixeble ó imitadora, creantse una lliteratura propia y á part de la castellana? (ix)

In this manifesto, Rubió highlights Catalonia's sense of inferiority with respect to the Castilian tradition and argues that Catalan writers must stop imitating Castilian ones. For Catalonia to gain its cultural independence, its writers must find their own voice. Highly influenced by Herderian theories on the relationship between language, national literatures and cultural identity, the *renaixentistes*, like Rubió, sought to "recover" their Catalanness which they saw as being buried under layers of Castilianisation. The aim of literature, for the *renaixentistes*, was to show Catalans who they were and to affirm their cultural distinctiveness. In this context, literature takes on an almost sacred role as preserver of Catalan culture and identity when the Catalans are faced with extreme difficulties.[2]

This role can clearly be seen during the Franco regime. To write in Catalan during this period was a political act, a means of expressing a point of view at odds with the regime's vision of "*España, una, grande y libre*". By writing about Catalonia under the Francoist yoke (and arrows), Catalan writers were – and are – able to explore the violence against Catalan culture and resist it.

For example, in *El temps de les cireres*, Montserrat Roig focuses on the initial repression of Catalan culture when Joan Miralpeix remembers how:

> Des del front enviava postals: 'Judit, estimada, com t'enyoro...' Però tot començà a capgirar-se quan, empresonat al camp de concentració de Betanzos, havia d'escriure amb una llengua que no era la seva: *'Querida Judit, recibí noticias de lo que sucedió a Esteban en Gualba, ¡cosas de los rojos! Afortunadamente, les queda poco para sus fechorías...'* [...] Calia regirar el pensament, calia començar a parlar d'una altra manera, vestir-se com ells volien, tancar-se a casa, [...] calia no sortir al carrer, car el carrer era d'ells [...] Calia anar a combregar i no riure obertament –tampoc no plorar–, cremar els llibres que els no agradaven, calia suposar que la teva llengua no valia per a res. (142–143)

This scene highlights the totalising nature of Francoist discourse. Joan is forced to act differently and to despise (at least outwardly) the things he holds dear, such as books and the Catalan language. The new Francoist order is built upon cultural, linguistic and political conformity and repression. The division between two world views is represented graphically, via the use of italics which mark Castilian as foreign, and linguistically, via the code-switching between the two languages. In the context of this passage, Catalan is associated with intimacy while Castilian – a language not his own – is representative of official discourse by its reference to "rojos".

Whilst Roig explores the most obvious moment of repression when one culture was silenced by another, Terenci Moix examines more insiduous forms of cultural repression in his generation-defining novel *El dia que va morir Marilyn*. The central theme of this novel is the recognition and recovery of personal and cultural identities. It is structured as a collective history told by two generations – those who lived through the Spanish Civil War and the first generation born after the war. The protagonists of the younger generation, Bruno and Jordi, reflect upon the cultural and social environment in which they have grown up and their reflections lead them to painful personal discoveries.

Like other bourgeois children of the post-War period, Bruno and Jordi are educated in Castilian which is considered *the* language of culture. Catalan, on the other hand, is treated very much as if it were a poor relation, somewhat of an embarrassment in social contexts. The acceptance of Castilian superiority by Jordi and Bruno is further influenced by the social conditioning and self-censorship against which Joan Miralpeix rails in *El temps de les cireres*. Bruno and his friends are discouraged from speaking Catalan outside the home because "si ens sentia la senyora Miralles podria dir a Lucita Bermejo de Pla que teníem molt poca finesa" (160). In such an environment it comes as no surprise that for Jordi and Bruno "aleshores la llengua [catalana] ens semblava molt lletja, i tot just podíem acceptar-la per parlar en família, en converses que no tenien cap mira intel·lectual" (160).

Bruno's acceptance of the superiority of Castilian culture is challenged when he reads Salvador Espriu's highly influential collection of poetry, *La pell de brau* (1960). The simple act of reading Espriu, according to Bruno:

> Se'ns despertava una passió tota nova, una possibilitat d'emoció a partir d'aquella realitat que encara portàvem dintre, ofegada des de feia molts anys, però no pas morta. Tota una tradició castellana que, des de petits, ens havien anat inculcant, rebutjà molt de temps, dintre nostre, l'antic somni de la terra dels pares. Si fins aleshores havíem cregut que tot allò que fos en català pudia a burgesia decadent, [...] una corrua de descobertes tan recents com a reconeixença de tot un poble, mena de martiri espriuenc sense les víctimes del qual nosaltres no hauríem existit. I vet aquí que, aquesta idea de poble, jo ja la sentia en català. (325–326)

Like Joan Miralpeix, Bruno's Catalan self is almost suffocated under the Francoist idea of Spanishness. However, unlike Joan, for Bruno, the superiority of Castilian over Catalan appears natural. He is unaware that the Castilian tradition with which he has grown up has impeded the discovery of his Catalan identity and, subsequently, his identification with a larger Catalan community. Upon making this discovery, Bruno comes to question everything he had previously thought about the world and to ultimately reject his Francoist education:

> Fins aleshores no se m'havia plantejat ni molt remotament el problema de pensar en una llengua i llegir i estudiar en una altra. [...] jo havia estat educat en una llengua que em condicionava, que em feia, en certa manera, allò que la llengua volia. Jo havia sentit parlar de les grans conquestes d'aquesta llengua estrangera [...] Tota la meva cultura m'havia estat transmesa amb paraules que no eren les mateixes del meu "cada dia". (326–327)

The contradictions Bruno suddenly becomes aware of can be described as typical of the postcolonial condition. He realises that language shapes who he is and, more importantly, that he was being taught the history and cultural norms of another language, which he now describes as foreign. This leads Bruno and Jordi to explore actively the history that their war-scarred parents had hidden from them.

The above texts seek to resist Castilian cultural, linguistic and literary domination in some way. As early as 1841, Rubió i Ors advances the idea of cultural independence by producing a Catalan-language literature which articulates cultural difference vis-à-vis a Castilian tradition. Well over a century later, Roig narrates the psychological damage caused by the Franco regime's enforced cultural and linguistic conformity. The cost of this conformity is clearly exposed in Moix's *El dia que va morir Marilyn*, in which the generation born after the war are inculcated with the values of the regime. For Bruno and Jordi, it is only through challenging established knowledge that Catalans can reject the cultural attitudes of a Castilian-centric society and heal their fractured identities.

Postcolonial Catalan Identities

In the face of the Franco regime's cultural "genocide", Catalan cultural and political discourses established firm borders between what is Catalan and what is not. These discourses emphasised Catalan homogeneity as a means of resisting cultural domination. Since the demise of the regime, the restored *Generalitat*, under Jordi Pujol, has set about creating a society in which all citizens identify primarily as Catalans. Political slogans, such as "És català tothom qui vui i treballa a Catalunya", and statements, such as "Excepte el que ve amb prejudicis anticatalans, l'immigrant, en principi, és un català" are indicative of this project (Termes 155). Such a project is not without its problems. As John McLeod argues, once-colonised countries run the risk of homogeneising diversity in the quest for unity against the imperial power (McLeod 103). A similar process can be seen to have occurred in Catalonia where the *Generalitat* has attempted to create a single national identity which subsumes social, political, geographical, cultural and linguistic differences. The journalist, Arcadi Espada, has criticised this homogeneising discourse in his book, *Contra Cataluña*, in which he argues that the Pujol-led government has associated itself so closely with the discourse of Catalanness that any criticism of it is not considered to be legitimate scrutiny expected in a democratic country but instead is treated as an assault "against Catalonia" itself.

The few studies of Catalonia from a postcolonial perspective tend to take for granted the nationalist formulation of Catalan culture and identity or they gloss over cultural diversity within Catalonia. The limiting of postcolonial studies to nationalist discourse is clearly seen in relation to the language question, especially as it pertains to literature. In her articles on the Catalan and Irish situations, Irene Boada argues that one of the major differences between their respective colonial experiences is that, despite their best efforts, in Ireland English is the principle language of communication and literary production whereas in Catalonia, Catalan is a vibrant language of literature, culture and daily use. Boada's articles exhibit a tension between Catalan nationalism and postcolonialism which becomes apparent when contrasting her treatment of the Irish and Catalan situations. In her analyses of short stories by Irish women writers, she argues that despite having to express themselves in the language of the colonisers, "the problem is not so much with the language per se, as with how the language is used" (Boada, "Nationalism" 18). Yet she makes no mention of whether this is valid for Esther Tusquets and Ana María Moix, the only two Castilian-language women writers from Catalonia she mentions in her first article (Boada, "Nationalism" 15). In fact, she only mentions in passing Catalans who choose to write in Castilian when she questions "pot la literatura en castellà ser literatura catalana?" (Boada, "Nacionalisme" 1). Palau Vergés similarly pays this issue little attention. On the one hand, she recognises the pluricultural nature of Catalan society, whilst on the other she states that Catalan literature is "la escrita en catalán" (174). In this definition,

Palau dismisses out of hand literary expressions by Catalans in languages other than Catalan.

Following Ashcroft et al., Boada and Palau interpret Catalan literature as an oppositional literature, that is to say one which resists Castilian cultural domination. This definition of postcolonial literature has received much criticism for "being essentially deconstructive and 'counter-discursive', [...] in perpetual confrontation with the master narrative of imperial discourse" (Schulze-Engler 320). Frank Shulze-Engler, for example, argues that interpreting postcolonial literatures in this fashion necessarily ties them into an on-going asymmetrical relationship with metropolitan culture and literature and does not allow them an agency of their own. In order to overcome the oppositional, but always subordinate role assigned to postcolonial literatures, Shulze-Engler argues that a "possible way out of this dilemma would be to place more emphasis on the *internal* histories of postcolonial societies, on the new challenges and problems that have arisen since independence was achieved" (323).

One literary text which confronts the internal divisions of Catalan society is Ignasi Riera's 1984 prize-winning novel, *El rellotge del pont d'Esplugues*. From the very beginning of the novel, Riera challenges the post-Francoist construction of Catalonia as an homogenous society. One character describes the narrative – the supposed diary of Rafaela – as an "homenatge negre a allò que tant odien els nostres dirigents: el país real" (9). This "país real" is Catalonia with all its defects, contradictions and divisions, including Castilian-speaking immigrants, workers, single mothers and poor Catalans. By suggesting that what is represented in the novel is "real", Riera suggests that official representations are fictitious and that they gloss over contradictions to create an image of a society which is far more united than it really is.

El rellotge... centres on the 1977 elections and the attempt by left-wing political activists to create a progressive and inclusive form of politics which would represent all Catalan citizens. The novel opens on 11 September 1976 – the first celebration of Catalonia's national day since the death of Franco. "*L'Onze de Setembre*" – the day Barcelona surrendered to the Bourbon army in 1714 – is symbolic of Catalan opposition to Castilian domination (Llobera 196–199). However, in *El rellotge...* the presence of immigrants upsets the neat division between us and them, vanquished and victors, colonised and colonisers which the day usually signifies. This challenge is expressed by one of the main characters, Antonio, who carries the Catalan and Andalusian flags sown back-to-back. Antonio defends his right to fly the Andalusian flag saying "Nadie me dirá que no sea andaluz. Nadie me lo puede decir. Nadie me robará el color a tierra que tiene la tierra en mi tierra [...] a mí que no me quitéis [...] el blanco y el verde de mi tierra, cosidas a la vuestra..." (31–32). By carrying the two flags, Antonio affirms his Andalusian past and Catalan present without denying the existence of either. The two flags are representative of the problem of social and cultural inclusion, as immigrants may feel erased or absent from a strictly Catalan cultural landscape, such as when, for example, the *senyera* alone is run up the flag pole. Antonio's defence highlights his fear of losing the culture which ties him to the land of his birth while not feeling entirely part of Catalan society and culture. While carrying the *senyera* during the *Diada* implies an identification with Catalan culture, for Antonio, this culture belongs exclusively to the Catalans and he does not feel a part of it. This is made clear in his use of the possessive pronouns "mi" and "vuestra". However, his attitude is rejected by the Catalan Lloveres, who responds to Antonio's statement "¿I què vol dir això de la *vuestra*? Que no ho és de teva, bonifacio?" (32). The attitudes expressed by Antonio and Lloveres are indicative of the limitations of seeing the day as a simple division between Catalonia and the rest of Spain, due the internal contradictions represented by Antonio's multiple identifications. Despite Lloveres's statement that the Catalan flag (and everything it symbolises) also belongs to Antonio, for this proud Andalusian immigrant, it does not represent sufficiently his different levels of identification with Catalonia and Andalusia. In Riera's hands, the *Onze de Setembre* is still a symbol of Catalan unity in the face of Castilian oppression but not at the cost of hiding Catalonia's internal divisions. In fact, Riera presents a situation in which unity can only be achieved via the recognition and acceptance of diversity.

Finding a means of fully incorporating immigrants within the symbolic Catalan community is a constant preoccupation in the novel. Instead of treating contact between what were (and still are) two cultures in negative terms, the novel seeks to open a "third space", as defined by Homi Bhabha. That is to say, a space which does not look to the past to show how these two cultures have changed or deviated from their "normal" state, rather a space which focuses on the future possibilities of a new identity (Bhabha 211). Riera attempts to overcome the marginalisation felt by immigrants in traditional Catalanist discourse by expanding it to embrace "'els altres', 'els nascuts a fora', 'els catalans d'adopció', 'els nou vinguts', 'els mal-anomenats xarnegos', [and] 'els andalusos-catalans'" (Riera 36).

In order to open up Catalan society to these new possibilities, the text tries to break down firmly entrenched ideas about what is and is not Catalan. The position taken by Antonio during the *Diada* is indicative of this attempt. However, the text does not just limit itself to challenging fixed notions of Catalan identity; recent attempts at constructing Catalan identities are also interrogated. For example, various characters throughout the novel question the inclusionist, but ultimately empty, rhetoric of the conservatively governed *Generalitat*. On one occasion, a minor character called Sánchez makes fun of the famous slogan "És català tothom qui viu i treballa a Catalunya", by focusing on the second prerequisite of Catalanness when he pointedly asks "¿y los que no trabajáis?" (Riera 49). By emphasising the connection between work and Catalan citizenship, Sánchez raises the issue of unemployment which demonstrates that there are other equally, if not more, important issues to resolve. In this context, political statements which attempt to forge a sense of community among all residents in Catalonia seem to fade into insignificance in a situation in which individuals do not have a job which would permit them to live with dignity. Given the complexity of the situation, *El rellotge...* does not attempt to furnish an easy solution to the issue of how to create solidarity without suppressing the multiple identities and interests of the citizens who make up contemporary Catalan society.

Conclusion[3]

In examining the historic ties between Catalonia and the Spanish State, we can see that the formation of the Spanish nation-state has involved the repression and denigration of cultures considered to be antithetical to national unity. By drawing on the concept of internal colonisation, it can be argued that Catalonia has suffered from a Spanish imperialism which sought to promote a single Spanish identity and culture, based largely on Castilian language and culture, throughout the entire state. In light of this situation, postcolonial approaches prove useful in furthering our understanding of cultural production from Catalonia. This is especially so if we take into account that the strategies Catalan writers have employed to resist cultural domination are similar to those used by writers from other countries which have experienced colonisation. However, Catalan postcolonial studies are still in their infancy and await detailed studies which go beyond the oppositional nature of postcolonial literatures and challenge nationalist formulations of cultural and identity (and literature) by exploring the multiple cultures and identities of Catalonia itself.

Works cited

Ashcroft, Bill, Gareth Griffiths, and Helen Tiffin. *The Empire Writes Back: Theory and Practice in Post-Colonial Literatures*. London: Routledge, 1989.

Barton, Simon. "The Roots of the National Question in Spain." *The National Question in Europe in Historical Context*. Eds. Mikulás Teich and Roy Porter. Cambridge: Cambridge University Press, 1993. 106–27.

Benet, Josep. *L'intent franquista de genocidi cultural contra Catalunya*. Barcelona: Publicacions de l'Abadia de Montserrat, 1995.

Bhabha, Homi. "The Third Space: Interview with Homi Bhabha." *Identity: Community, Culture, Difference*. Ed. Jonathan Rutherford. London: Lawrence & Wishart, 1990. 207–21.

Boada, Irene. "Nacionalisme i llengua en el conte contemporani català i irlandès. Algunes perspectives feministes i postcolonials." *Journal of Catalan Studies / Revista Internacional de Catalanística* 2 (1999). http://www.uoc.es/jocs/2/articles/ boada/ index.html

——. "Nationalism and Language in Catalan and Irish Contemporary Short Stories: Feminist and Postcolonial Perspectives." *Catalan Review: International Journal of Catalan Culture* 12.1 (1998): 9–21.

Boyd, Carolyn P. "History, Politics, and Culture, 1936–1975." *The Cambridge Companion to Modern Spanish Culture*. Ed. David T. Gies. Cambridge: Cambridge University Press, 1999. 86–103.

Brooker, Peter. *A Concise Glossary of Cultural Theory*. London: Arnold, 1999.

Conversi, Daniele. *The Basques, the Catalans and Spain: Alternative Routes to Nationalist Mobilisation*. London: Hurst & Company, 1997.

Crameri, Kathryn. *Language, the Novelist and National Identity in Post-Franco Catalonia*. Oxford: Legenda, 2000.

Elliott, J.H. *Imperial Spain: 1469–1716*. London: Penguin, 1970.

Espada, Arcadi. *Contra Catalunya. Una crónica*. Barcelona: Flor de Viento, 1997.

Franco Bahamonde, Francisco. *Palabras del caudillo. 19 abril 1937–31 diciembre 1938*. Barcelona: Fe, 1939.

Gilbert, Helen, and Joanne Tompkins. *Post-Colonial Drama: Theory, Practice, Politics*. London: Routledge, 1996.

Hechter, Michael. *Internal Colonialism: The Celtic Fringe in British National Development, 1536–1966*. Berkeley: University of Calfornia Press, 1975.

Jorba, Manuel. "Actituds davant de la llengua en relació amb la Renaixença." *Actes del sisè col·loqui internacional de llengua i literatura catalanes, Roma, 28 setembre – 2 octubre 1982*. Eds. Giuseppe Tavani and Jordi Pinell. Barcelona: Publicacions de l'Abadia de Montserrat, 1982. 127–51.

King, Stewart. "Orquestando la identidad: estrategias poscoloniales en *L'òpera quotidiana* de Montserrat Roig." *Proceedings of the First Symposium on Catalonia in Australia / Actes del primer simposi sobre Catalunya a Austràlia / Actas del primer simposio sobre Cataluña en Australia (La Trobe University, Melbourne, 27–29 September 1996)*. Eds. Robert Archer and Emma Martinell Gifre. Barcelona: PPU, 1998. 59–76.

——. "Transformando el estado Español: los discursos centrípeto y centrífugo en la literatura catalana de expresión castellana." *Ixquic: Revista Hispánica Internacional de Análisis y Creación* 1 (1999): 23–36.

Lleal, Coloma. *Breu història de la llengua catalana*. Barcelona: Barcanova, 1992.

Llobera, Josep R. "The Role of Commemoration in (Ethno)Nation-Building. The Case of Catalonia." *Nationalism and the Nation in the Iberian Peninsula: Competing and Conflicting Identities*. Eds. Clare Mar-Molinero and Ángel Smith. Oxford: Berg, 1996. 191–206.

Mañé i Flaquer, Joan. *Colección de artículos*. Barcelona: Antoni Brusi, 1857.

McClintock, Anne. "The Angel of Progress: Pitfalls of the Term 'Postcolonialism'." *Colonial Discourse / Postcolonial Theory*. Eds. Francis Barker, Peter Hulme and Margaret Iversen. Manchester: Manchester University Press, 1994. 253–66.

McLeod, John. *Beginning Postcolonialism*. Manchester: Manchester University Press, 2000.

McPhee, Peter. "A Case-Study of Internal Colonization: The *Francisation* of Northern Catalonia." *Review* 3.3 (1980): 399–428.

Moix, Terenci. *El dia que va morir Marilyn. Edició definitiva*. Barcelona: Edicions 62, 1995.

Murray, Stuart, and Alan Riach. "A Questionnaire." *SPAN* 41 (1995): 6–64.

O'Donnell, Hugh. "Recounting the Nation: The Domestic Catalan *Telenovela*." *Cultura Popular: Studies in Spanish and Latin American Popular Culture*. Eds. Shelley

Godsland and Anne M. White. Oxford: Peter Lang, 2002. 243–261.

Palau Vergés, Montserrat. "Autoras catalanas: doble marginación y doble rebelión (género y nacionalismo en Cataluña)." *Identidades multiculturais: revisión dos discursos teóricos*. Eds. Ana Bringas López and Belén Martín Lucás. Vigo: Universidade de Vigo, 2000. 169–76.

Preston, Paul. *Franco: A Biography*. London: Fontana, 1995.

Riera, Ignasi. *El rellotge del pont d'Esplugues*. Barcelona: Planeta, 1984.

Roig, Montserrat. *El temps de les cireres*. Barcelona: Edicions 62, 1977.

Rubió i Ors, Joaquim. *Lo gayté del Llobregat. Poesias de don Joaquim Rubió y Ors*. Barcelona: Estampa de Joseph Rubio, 1841.

Said, Edward W. *Culture and Imperialism*. London: Chatto and Windus, 1993.

Samsó, Joan. *La cultura catalana. Entre la clandestinitat i la represa pública*. Vol. 1. Barcelona: Publicacions de l'Abadia de Montserrat, 1994.

Schulze-Engler, Frank. "Beyond Post-Colonialism: Multiple Identities in East African Literature." *Us/Them: Translation, Transcription and Identity in Post-Colonial Literary Cultures*. Ed. Gordon Collier. Amsterdam: Rodopi, 1992. 319–28.

Termes, Josep. *La immigració a Catalunya i altres estudis d'història del nacionalisme català*. Barcelona: Empúries, 1984.

Notes

[1] It is important to distinguish between a decree and its effectiveness. The fact that some of the above laws were largely ignored can be seen in the repeated banning of the teaching of Catalan in schools. The need to articulate repeatedly these laws demonstrates, according to Coloma Lleal, that they were frequently broken (117).

[2] Although literature is still considered to play a critical role in preserving Catalanness, it has largely been overtaken by mass media, such as television. For a throrough analysis of the role of television in promoting Catalan culture see O'Donnell (2002).

[3] The subheadings which structure this article – colonisation, resistance and postcolonial Catalan identities – appear to confirm Anne McClintock's criticism that postcolonial theories are predicated upon notions of linear development in which a people progress from colonisation, passing through postcolonialism, to "enlightened hybridity" (253–254). Such a structuring device is, of course, artificial and the headings used in this article are not meant to suggest that there is a clear cut division between the categories. For example, the fact that Catalonia, since its conception, has been crossed by categories of class, gender, sexuality, region and ethnicity puts paid to the argument that multiple identities are only a characteristic of postcolonial societies. Furthermore, the very idea that Catalonia be considered a postcolonial country is questionable because, for some Catalans "there may be nothing 'post' about colonialism at all" as Catalonia, like the Basque Country and Galicia, are locked into a subordinate political relationship with the Spanish State (McClintock 256).

(Un)common Ground? A Comparative Genealogy of British and Latin American Cultural Studies

Jeff Browitt

> Is there a way of thinking of and engaging recent [Latin American] cultural production and processes of state re-formation that can account not just for the historical transition to transnationalism but also for the possible definition of future political communities and commonalities?
> (Gareth Williams 9)

Williams asks his question in relation to the crisis in Latin American discourses of national development and revolutionary nationalism, as these collapse within the context of triumphant neo-liberal global capitalism. By implication, the question includes Williams himself as an interlocutor and fellow-traveller in any such future commonalities. But are such theorisations about Latin America, indeed the proposing of solutions to Latin American crises from the perspective of a non-Latin American "outsider", legitimate? If British-born cultural critics like Jean Franco, Jon Beasley-Murray, John Kraniauskis, William Rowe and Gareth Williams, who are also Latin Americanists, take as their object of analysis Latin American culture(s), are they British or Latin American cultural critics, or a hybrid of both, and does it matter? Are British cultural studies the study of culture in Britain, or simply any cultural studies conducted by British-born cultural theorists, or a cultural studies that begins from premises developed within British intellectual culture? Similarly, are Latin American cultural critics simply those who were born in Latin America, or those who take Latin American culture as their object of study, or both? Are Latin American cultural studies a homegrown product, or another foreign imposition, or a hybrid critical intellectual practice? In other words, does one's country of origin, or one's object of study or indeed the country of origin of the cultural theory itself, determine how the person or the study is classified and thus the study's legitimacy? These questions would appear to have profound significance for some, since the "politics of location" have in recent times come to centre-stage in debates over "Latin Americanism".[1] These are some of the issues this paper seeks to address.

The term "Latin Americanism" is usefully defined by Alberto Moreiras at the end of his introduction to *The Exhaustion of Difference* as "the sum total of engaged representations concerning Latin America as an object of knowledge". He goes on to declare that, at least in his case, he makes "no general distinctions between work produced in the north and work produced in the south (distinctions can be made but they can never be general)" (24). The point Moreiras wishes to make is one against the fetishisation of location. He acknowledges that the work carried out by non-Latin American Latin Americanists is always problematically installed within the hegemonic apparatuses of metropolitan universities and the "privileges of Northern knowledge" (or for that matter, installed in a university in any country that is primarily European). Nonetheless, Moreiras is bemused by those Latin American Latin Americanists who take solace in a "dubious legitimation in the positing of location as final redemption" (6) and who regard outsiders (typically North American interlocutors) as mired in "unredeemable ignorance", especially when the historical complaint has always been that Latin Americans have *themselves* been traditionally banished to "unredeemable ignorance" by Northern knowledges because of *their* outsider status vis-à-vis their geo-political location. Abril Trigo makes essentially the same point: "a compelling critique of US Latin Americanism is only legitimate on condition of a concomitant problematization of homemade Latin Americanism. The epistemological borders don't disappear because the intellectual happens to write from Montevideo instead of Pittsburgh" (87).

I have begun this paper by highlighting the politics of location simply because I see it as a symptom of a much deeper malaise, even if not consciously recognised or articulated as such: the collapse of the two-century long dream of independent Latin American nation-states attaining relative parity with the developed world and where to apportion blame for this failure. Because of a historical frustration that will not speak its name, those who bring "outside" theories or come from an institutional location outside of Latin America are criticised as "neo-colonial" or "imperialist". Against this assumption, this paper will carry out a brief genealogy of both what is commonly regarded as British cultural studies and Latin American cultural studies as a way of establishing possible (un)common ground between British or Latin American cultural studies, rather than the automatic presumption that anything European is necessarily a Trojan horse of cultural imperialism for Latin Americans. It will also hopefully contribute to overcoming what I regard as, at base, a divisive and ultimately futile turf war in the name of academic prestige.

British cultural studies

British cultural studies is most typically associated with the Birmingham Centre for Cultural Studies, originally opened in 1964 under the directorship of Richard Hoggart and which only recently (2002) closed, another victim of the neoliberal restructuring of British Higher Education. Being the dominant institutional moment of British cultural studies, both in Britain and internationally, for most of the 1970s and 1980s, the Centre's work typically stands in for a definition of cultural studies. While there was never a single Birmingham model, but rather an inescapable plurality of competing and often contradictory models, nevertheless the cumulative logic of British cultural studies after Stuart Hall took over the directorship has been in the direction of a sociology of mass media. But this is not the only prominent strand of British cultural studies. If we define cultural studies as a practice that seeks to theorise the antithesis between culture and capitalist industrial modernity, then the genealogy of British cultural studies can be traced back through a "culturalist" tradition beginning at least as far back as Mathew Arnold and passing through T. S. Eliot and F. R. Leavis, before its later subversion and "popularisation" by "left culturalism" in the shape of the New Left cultural critics, E. P. Thompson, Richard Hoggart and Raymond Williams. Williams's "cultural materialism" would subsequently effect a synthesis between this "left culturalism" and "Western Marxism", an orientation itself later challenged and decentred by Hall's structuralist intervention. Let us briefly look at each moment.

A central motif in culturalist theory is that of a necessary antithesis between culture and civilisation, or more accurately, "between the authenticity of natural, lived 'experience' and the mechanistic imperatives of industrialisation, [which] clearly attest to the pain and the trauma of the very first industrial revolution, that which occurred in Britain itself" (Milner and Browitt 26). In 1869, Mathew Arnold published *Culture and Anarchy*, in which culture, understood as the essentially disinterested pursuit of beauty and harmony, is counterposed to utilitarian, material civilisation and the blight of industrial modernisation. But who would guarantee this type of anti-utilitarian culture? Arnold rejected in turn the "Barbarian" aristocracy, the "Philistine" middle class and the working-class "Populace", the latter "raw and half-developed [...] half-hidden amidst its poverty and squalor" (Arnold 101–5). It thus devolved to the cultured "remnant" within each class, "the intelligentsia", to sustain the continued development of human culture: "persons who are mainly led, not by their class spirit, but by a general *humane* spirit, by the love of human perfection" (109). While all could not consciously understand this ideal of cultured perfection, it could nevertheless be inculcated as an ideal to aspire to through the expansion of state-sponsored education. Such education would thus bolster a set of ideal cultural values to act as a counterweight to anarchy and disorder: "without order there can be no society, and without society there can be no human perfection" (203). Clearly, anarchy emanates from the "working class". Arnold's defence of culture thus becomes a defence of elite cultural taste in which the autonomous lettered intelligentsia, the "remnant", will henceforth legislate the national "tradition". T. S. Eliot and F. R. Leavis would subsequently come to develop roughly analogous Arnoldian positions on culture. These included a totalistic and organicist conception of culture, embracing both the literary and the non-literary, but ultimately reaching its highest level in the literary tradition; culture as the bearer of essential moral values over and against the anomie and disintegration of capitalist modernity;

and one of the fundamental tropes of anti-utilitarian romanticism: its enduring cultural pessimism and abhorrence of "mass" society (Milner and Browitt 25–32).

The rise of what we more properly regard as modern British cultural studies began to emerge in the 1950s in the context of a European-wide disenchantment with a certain form of left-wing politics, itself related to changes in the objective socio-economic conditions of the period and to a changed conception of aesthetics and culture. The 1950s heralded a loss of faith by many on the European Left with authoritarian, centralised Leftism, best exemplified in the Soviet Union with the gulag and in the rigidity of Communist parties all over the world. But there was also a need to explain the acceptance of capitalism, which had managed to survive the Great Depression. Part of the explanation lay in the manufacture of consensus such that the ruling classes can continue to rule without overtly coercive measures. Part of the solution was obviously the creation of the welfare state, which in Western industrialized countries reached its golden period in the 1950s and 1960s. But part of the explanation also lay in the ability to control the populace through mass media and educational institutions, which ensured a compliant citizenry. Though Gramsci was not yet a theoretical source for the British culturalists, they nevertheless sensed that capitalist values might also be challenged in the cultural sphere by getting involved in working-class culture and political agitation, in adult education, and by challenging the humanist tradition in intellectual and artistic discourse, which had historically been complicit with elite control and conservatism and whose literary manifestation was the tradition of British "culturalism" from Arnold to Leavis.

Culture thus became centrally important and this is the focus that Williams, Thompson and Hoggart brought to left-wing critique. Here the elite concept of culture, the culture of the Sunday supplements, is displaced by a much broader sense of culture as a terrain of class struggle. In *The Making of the English Working Class*, Thompson foregrounded the "heroic culture" of the early English working class, which he compared to Romantic anti-utilitarianism. For his part, Richard Hoggart in *The Uses of Literacy* decentres "literature" into "culture", combining an ethnographic account of Yorkshire working-class culture with Leavisite practical criticism of mass media texts: "The old forms of class culture are in danger of being replaced by a poorer kind of classless [...] culture [...] and this is to be regretted" (Hoggart 343). Hoggart valorises working-class culture in contradistinction to Leavis's "sensitive minority", but only to lament its passing.

This type of left culturalism reached its fullest analytical range in Raymond Williams's cultural materialism. Like Hoggart, Williams valued working-class culture positively and, like Eliot and Leavis, still retained an anthropological and organicist sense of culture as "not only a body of intellectual and imaginative work; it is also and essentially a whole way of life" (*Culture and*

Society 311). But Williams would importantly add the "collective democratic institution" to his sense of culture, including trade unions, co-operatives and working class political parties (313), thus effecting a common culture made up of a plurality of class cultures, in which the distinction between "bourgeois and working-class culture" is that between "alternative ideas of the nature of social relationships" (311). For Williams, the antithesis of middle-class individualism was no longer the minority culture of the intelligentsia, but rather proletarian solidarity: "In its definition of the common interest as true self-interest, in its finding of individual verification primarily in the community, the idea of solidarity is potentially the real basis of society" (318). Since a common culture is not yet really common, Williams would come to displace the common culture from an idealised, class-divided past, to an as yet unformed utopian future (*Revolution*).

Though the idea of class cultures was important for Williams, he was nevertheless careful not to reduce art to class, inventing the notion of "structure of feeling" to try to account for "the culture of a period [which] is the particular living result of all the elements in the general organization" (64). This also marks the moment when Williams becomes increasingly interested in "Western Marxism", the tradition of "critical" Marxism that developed in Germany, Italy and France, as distinct from official Marxism of the Communist Party. Like the culturalist tradition, its characteristic thematics were human agency, subjective consciousness and also culture. But it was through Antonio Gramsci in particular that Williams was able to theorise how it is that structures of feeling can be common to different classes, and yet nonetheless represent the interests of a particular class. Here the Gramscian concept of "hegemony" is chosen over both "culture" and "ideology", since it provides a Marxist theory of legitimation: in place of the orthodox Marxist base/superstructure theory, Gramsci proposes a civil society/political society model, thus connecting politico-economic coercion with legitimation in the maintenance of social stability: "State = political society + civil society, in other words hegemony protected by the armour of coercion" (263). The term hegemony here refers to the permeation throughout the whole of society of a system of values and beliefs that support the existing ruling class.

For Williams, Gramsci's central achievement was to show how culture as ideology is central to the workings of social domination (*Marxism* 117–120). Williams thus insisted that culture is itself both real and material: "From castles and palaces and churches to prisons and workhouses and schools ... from weapons of war to a controlled press [...] These are never superstructural activities. They are necessarily material production" (93). Hence too his concept of "cultural materialism" as a "theory of culture as a (social and material) productive process and of specific practices, of 'arts', as social uses of material means of production (from language as material 'practical consciousness' to the specific technologies of writing and forms of writing, through to mechanical and electronic communications systems)" (*Problems* 243). Like Gramsci, and like contemporary Latin American cultural theorists, Williams was concerned with the problem of counter-hegemony: those moments in the interstices of power and control from where a genuinely democratic and alternative culture might emerge to challenge capitalist hegemony. The cultural materialist approach to cultural studies would become influential in literary and cultural studies ranging from New Historicism to feminism, with perhaps its most distinguished practitioner after Williams being Terry Eagleton.

Whilst cultural materialism was mainly concerned with applying "post-culturalist" forms of analysis to literary studies, the roughly equivalent approach to the study of popular culture was that developed, in the first place, as "Cultural Studies" at the University of Birmingham. Excluded from "English" by Leavisism, "the popular" had become the subject matter of the new proto-discipline of cultural studies largely at the instigation of Williams and Hoggart themselves. Hoggart became Director of the new Centre for Contemporary Cultural Studies in 1964. Williams's own contribution was a critique of existing mass media institutions and texts in *Communications* (1962) and *Television: Technology and Cultural Form* (1974). Both books sought to identify the institutional forms that could sustain a properly democratic communications system. Thus the new televisual technologies were, in Williams's opinion, "the contemporary tools of the long revolution towards an educated and participatory democracy" (*Television* 151).

When Hoggart left Birmingham in 1968, he was succeeded by Stuart Hall, the latter still very much under the influence of Williams's left culturalist argument. Under Hall, the Centre shifted its focus almost exclusively to popular culture. Hall himself had previously co-authored *The Popular Arts* with Paddy Whannel, a study which dealt directly with problems of "value and evaluation" in the study of popular culture. Like Williams and Hoggart, Hall and Whannel were concerned with rescuing what was valuable and creative in "popular art" from its denigration as "mass" culture. This kind of theoretical culturalism continued to remain in play at the Birmingham Centre. It is particularly evident, for example, in the Centre's work on youth subcultures, where an ethnographic focus was combined with an emphasis on generation and class deriving in part from Williams, so as to produce accounts of sub-cultural resistance to the dominant culture (Hall and Jefferson).

The shift to popular culture was accompanied by a turn to semiology and processes of "signification" as the Centre became fascinated by structuralist and later post-structuralist thematics. Hall's own work tended to focus on the mass media, especially as these construct public opinion and, in effect, police those popular subcultural practices and subversions that might threaten the state's legitimacy. The precise point at which Hall's structuralist-semiological turn began to diverge from culturalism is difficult to document. By 1980, however, Hall published the seminal essay, "Cultural studies: two paradigms". Here, "culturalism" was no longer the obviously available starting point for the would-be discipline, but rather only one of two competing paradigms, each with its attendant strengths and weaknesses. For Hall, "culture" in Williams and "experience" in Thompson were seen as performing fundamentally analogous theoretical functions, that is, they denoted simultaneously, and thereby elided the distinction between, active consciousness on the one hand, and relatively "given", determinate conditions on the other. The result was a theoretical humanism, with two distinguishing characteristics: experience and creativity. Hall's response to this "empiricism" was to insist that: "Analysis must deconstruct [...] 'lived wholeness' in order to be able to think its determinate conditions" ("Cultural" 62).

Hall enumerates the various strengths of the structuralist model: its emphasis on the constraining effects of pre-existent structures on human activity; its conception of unity-in-difference, rather than a totality of homologous and corresponding structures; and finally, its emphasis on the need for a theory of ideology to complement the culturalist focus on experience, since ideology provides the legitimating mechanism for the perpetuation of relations of domination and subordination between classes. Culturalism's strength, on the other hand, is its belief in the ongoing capacity for active, collective resistance to oppressive structures, that is, the capacity for conscious organisation in making one's own history. Hall sees both paradigms as complementary in the sense that taken together they unite the opposite poles of creative activity and the constraining or determinate structures within which human beings are required to act: "between them [...] they address what must be the *core problem* of Cultural Studies ... the dialectic between conditions and consciousness" ("Cultural" 72).

Nevertheless, the logic of Hall's argument, according to Milner and Browitt, "leaves culturalism with remarkably little to do. In truth, Hall's was an anti-culturalist argument, its effects all the more damaging for its professed evenhandedness" (52). The Birmingham Centre thus moved from a conception of "meaning (as an activity of human beings) to signification (as an operation of language)" (Peck 212). It also repeated one of the founding tropes of structuralism, most recognizable in the work of Lévi-Strauss: "language/culture is not substance, but form. Culture was not the content of expression or experience, but the codes, inventories, taxonomies, (i.e. the principles of formation) that provided the frameworks and basis for thought/consciousness" (Peck 217). The logic of this theoretical reformulation would lead a decade later to the abandonment of "metaphors of transformation" and the "radical imaginary" which "no longer command assent" in favour of a new metaphor which imagines cultural politics as a thinking of the "relations between the 'social' and 'the symbolic'" (Hall, "Metaphors" 287–88). In a characteristically Althusserian move, Hall posits the relative autonomy of the superstructure, thus occluding any engagement with the productive base (a more totalistic materialist understanding of the relation between culture and political economy), to avoid the claim of Marxist reductionism (economism). This separation into different spheres (the autonomous superstructure – language, culture, signification, subjectivity – versus the economy) goes against Hall's own earlier claim of the need to think a "non-reductive determinacy" ("Cultural" 72). As Peck insists, this repeats Thompson's early distinction between "raw materials of life experience" and the "disciplines and systems" which "handle, transmit or distort it":

> [B]ut, contra to Thompson, [Hall] treats their relation as arbitrary rather than necessary. Ironically this strategy conserves both idealism and economism – those twin pillars of modern thought – by making culture the exclusive domain of thought, language, and meaning, and turning the economic into a realm of mute, non-signifying materiality. (242)

Hall's work has been hugely influential in international cultural studies (especially in its US and Australian variants) and cannot be reduced to a mere distraction from Williamsite cultural materialism. It nevertheless took cultural studies away from political economy and in the direction of the so-called politics of identity and representation (race, ethnicity, feminism, gay and lesbian studies, and so forth). Perhaps the best way to come to terms with this historic shift is by regarding it as "the politics we had to have", a labour of "clearing out", especially in relation to a certain form of dogmatic cultural leftism that had exhausted its analytical productivity because of its inability to come to terms with sexism and patriarchal discourse, with non-European cultures, with homophobia, and so forth. As John Higgins insists, even in the work of such an admirable cultural critic as Raymond Williams, these areas of critique were simply not discussed:

> Despite the claims of his later work, Williams signally fails to engage directly enough with the work of his structuralist and post-structuralist antagonists, while his positive notions of identity, social rootedness and community owe too much to, and are ultimately compromised by, their own roots in conservative thought [...] he appears to be constitutively blind to the politics of race and gender, and the dynamics of imperialism. (170).

To be fair to Williams, these never really were his object of study. Nevertheless, the criticism still stands. If the Birmingham Centre's legacy has been to facilitate critique of these latter forms of domination, then in this it should be defended.

What, then, are "cultural studies"? Most obviously, the academic study of "culture". The word "culture" itself can be usefully defined as "the entire range of institutions, artifacts and practices that make up our symbolic universe" and that would include "art and religion, science and sport, education and leisure, but not normally economics or politics" (Milner and Browitt 228), though these latter are both implicated in culture in a fundamental way. Culture in this sense is not limited to a "cultured" sense of culture: what you might find in the Sunday supplements or in art galleries, for instance. No strict consensus yet exists for defining "cultural studies", however, nor how to organise such a study. But some key characteristics that double for both British and Latin American cultural studies can be posited. Firstly, cultural studies can be conceived as an inter-, trans- or post-disciplinary practice, especially in the intersection of sociology and anthropology, literary theory and philosophy, and the "deconstruction" of the disciplinary boundaries that have traditionally demarcated literature from fiction, art from culture, elite from popular. Secondly, cultural studies can be defined as a *political* pedagogical practice (cultural Leftism) meant to interrupt conventional academic disciplines, most typically literature departments, canonical texts and any hegemonic genres of cultural discourse. Finally, cultural studies raises popular culture to the level of a valid object of intellectual enquiry.

Latin American cultural studies

A genealogy of Latin American writing about culture would need to begin at least as far back as Simón Bolívar's *Carta de Jamaica* (1816) and his vision of Latin America on the eve of independence, and Andrés Bello, the educator and poet, whose *Silvas americanas* (1820s) are one of the first celebrations of purely American themes. Similarly, in the mid-nineteenth century, Domingo Faustino Sarmiento and his notorious civilization/ barbarism trope inaugurated a long-standing and still topical debate about Europeanism versus Americanism. As we have seen, British cultural studies grew out of a so-called "culturalist" tradition, whose most generally defining features were "a stress on human agency and creativity and a commitment to the positive value of a 'common culture', often understood as both national in character and reaching its highest form in 'art'" (Browitt and Milner 55). If we substitute "continental" for "national", we see a remarkably similar stance in "Arielism", as defined by José Enrique Rodó, and "*modernismo*" as it was conceived, among others, by Rubén Darío and José Martí around the turn of the nineteenth century, in opposition to the alleged obsessive materialism of the United States.

Rodó, in particular, appeals to the figure of Ariel from Shakespeare's play, *The Tempest*, as representative of a Latin cultural-aesthetic spirituality that acts as a bulwark against utilitarian and imperialising culture from the north. Julio Ramos describes this spirituality as "a critique of '[North-] Americanization', which Rodó placed in opposition to the alternative of a legacy and archive inspired by the invention of Euro-American Latinism" (246). A resistant manifesto nevertheless becomes a hegemonic and self-validating move by positing the centrality of the *letrado* as the voice of the "people": "the practices of Latin-Americanist mediation [Martí and Rodó] in both cases are based on the varied inflections of a cultural-aesthetic authority that privileges the role of literature in the construction of citizenship, or what Schiller has called 'the aesthetic education of man'" (Ramos 246). Furthermore, Rodó reacted against what he negatively termed "cosmopolitanism [...] synonymous with foreign influences and related to a popular and working-class immigration that threatened the very integrity of Latin American 'high culture'" (Ramos 246).[2] The dislike of "cosmopolitanism" was no doubt also related to what Rodó regarded as decadentism in Darío's taste for all things French and foreign, a criticism itself not unrelated to struggles for cultural capital within the nascent autonomous field of Latin American literature (see Browitt, "Modernismo").

In the early twentieth century, essayists like Alfonso Reyes, Pedro Henríquez Ureña and José Vasconcelos, who often combined the roles of literary critic, publicist, public intellectual, politician or political activist, continued this tradition of culturalist *letrado*. Still later, the poetry and essays of Octavio Paz, the reflections on Cuban national culture and its transcultural nature by Fernando Ortiz in *Contrapunteo cubano* (1970), and the reworking of Marxist ideas adjusted to the realities and particularities of Andean socio-cultural histories by José Carlos Mariátegui's *Siete ensayos de interpretación de la realidad peruana* (1928), were all prominent expressions of cultural self-reflexivity. But what most of these sorts of intellectual thought on culture shared was a homogenising and un-theorised, optimistic assumption that the "national" or "continental" is the ultimate framework of analysis, and that the lettered intellectual can unproblematically stand in for the heterogeneous ethnicities, races and classes which make up *"Nuestra América"*, *"el continente mestizo"*, *"la raza cósmica"*, *"el mestizaje cultural"*, and so forth.

Latin American cultural studies in their contemporary form first began to emerge in the 1960s and 1970s, due to two principal factors: firstly, the success of the Cuban Revolution and the continental-wide movement towards "decolonised" and "revolutionary" cultural expression; and secondly, the growing influence of European critical and cultural theories that read capitalist modernity through culture, as these combine and hybridise with a Latin American tradition of thinking about culture. The following are some representative theorists and their work: José María Arguedas and Antonio Cornejo Polar on the clash of indigenous and mestizo cultures in Peru; Roberto Fernández Retamar on the inversion of the image of Caliban as a liberatory gesture vis-à-vis European and US imperialism; Ángel Rama, firstly on the notion of literary transculturation, and then on the role of lettered intellectuals in the construction of the modern liberal nation-state; still later, Carlos Monsiváis on urban popular culture in Mexico, Néstor García Canclini on cultural hybridity and the nexus between consumer cultures and citizenship; Jesús Martín-Barbero on the cultural politics of media and entertainment industries; Beatriz Sarlo on Argentine peripheral modernity; Nelly Richard and Martin Hopenhaym in relation to post-dictatorial cultural production; Hugo Achugar and Mabel Moraña on literary decolonization; Xavier Albó on Bolivian culture; Ileana Rodríguez on gender and ethnicity in post-colonial Latin American literatures by women; Marc Zimmerman on Central American revolutionary culture and *testimonio*; William Rowe on cultural poetics; Jean Franco on just about everything; Walter Mignolo on "colonial difference;" Julio Ramos on Latin American modernity and the institutional history of national literatures; Roberto Schwarz on "misplaced [European] ideas" and cultural imitation in Brazil; Doris Sommer on the foundational romances of nineteenth-century literature and on *testimonio*; Josefina Ludmer on the promotion of the national-popular through gauchesque literature; and so forth. This list of cultural studies theorists and practitioners and their objects of study is by no means exhaustive. Whether they be literary, cultural, media or urban anthropological studies, what tends to unite them is their significance as a series of sustained reflections on the nature of cultural modernisation, and later postmodernisation, in a period subject to profound economic, political and cultural change: military dictatorship in the Southern Cone countries; civil war in Central America in the 1980s; debt crisis; neoliberal privatisation and the dismantling of the (always tenuous) welfare state; the globalisation of the new media technologies; and the politics of difference (feminism, anti-racism, indigenous rights, non-normative sexualities, and so forth).

It is during this period and in direct relation to these socio-economic, political and cultural changes, that the Latin American nation-states enter into crisis in its dual political and cultural dimensions: the "state", as the legal, administrative, and military expression of the cultural "nation". When either enters into crisis – the delegitimisation of the state or a crisis in national cultural identity – it inevitably draws the other into crisis as well. This is also the moment of crisis in the hermeneutic authority of intellectuals and academics, who are obliged to adjust their function, in Zigmunt Bauman's phrase, "from legislators to interpreters". I therefore use the term Latin American cultural studies to cover a wide variety of trends, three of the most important of which are "cultural studies", "subaltern/postcolonial studies", and "cultural critique". Few theorists fit neatly into any one of the preceding categories; indeed there is substantial overlap in the theoretical starting points and objects of study and certainly in the generally Leftist progressive politics that animate their projects. I will begin, then, by referring to the representative work of a few practitioners of cultural studies and then see how these differ from subaltern studies and cultural critique.

Cultural Studies

Jesús Martín-Barbero's work, for example, is a sophisticated engagement with communications studies, culture, politics and history within the context of Latin America's problematic relationship with modernity. He cites European cultural theorists as his first and most important inspiration in cultural studies: firstly Gramsci and Benjamin, then Thompson, Williams and Hoggart, and then de Certeau, Hall and Foucault, though the Argentine critic, José Luis Romero, is cited as a theorist who "marked my work very deeply" (Martín-Barbero, "Interview" 223). In his most famous work, *De los medios a las mediaciones* (1987), he inverts traditional theorising on the mass-mediated construction of cultural identity by pointing out that the mass media are not the source of mass society, but merely an aspect (albeit highly important) of the massification of society that was already underway by the end of the nineteenth century: "the historical constitution of mass society, rather than being linked to the degradation of culture by the media, is linked to the long, slow process in the development of national markets, states and cultures, and to the patterns which in this process caused popular memory to enter into complicity with the mass imaginary" (114). It is in this sense that Martín-Barbero theorises the role of the mass media in the construction of a national polity and culture as a "kind of 'deviant modernity', which most people in Latin America enter not through the book, but through the narratives produced by the audiovisual culture industry: cinema, radio, television, video-games and music videos" ("Interview" 225–6).

Another prominent and representative figure of so-called *estudios culturales* is Nestor García Canclini, an Argentine anthropologist who has worked for many years in the Universidad Autónoma Metropolitana de México. García Canclini's work has found inspiration not only in local tradition, but also in the theories of Deleuze, Bhabha, Hall and Williams. His work has ranged over the hybrid border culture of the United States and Mexico, particularly the city of Tijuana, and indigenous and *mestizo* communities, as these are involved in the production and marketing of craftwork. One of his primary concerns is to think culture and consumption together. In *Culturas híbridas: Estrategias para entrar y salir de la modernidad* (1989), he set himself the task of studying popular culture in the light of the transformations that craftwork and traditional popular *fiestas* have undergone with the impact of capitalist modernity. This leads García Canclini to a theory of "cultural reconversion": popular cultures do not necessarily die with the onset of modernity, they go somewhere else, they are fashioned into something new, as a necessity of survival. This also involves processes of cultural mixing and "hybridization". In fact, according to García Canclini, this is the only kind of culture there is and has always been. This conception frees us, he believes, from the now discredited notions of cultural purity and cultural authenticity, which have traditionally been enlisted to determine such ideological constructs as national identity. He claims that processes of cultural reconversion and refashioning of craftwork, rather than mere accommodation or adaptation to European or North American market perspectives, demonstrate that popular artisans can take part in the global cultural scene and that this situation has therefore an empowering effect on their lives.

This concern with the nexus between culture and economy has led García Canclini to a series of sustained reflections on civil society and citizenship and their intersection with consumption in *Consumidores y ciudadanos: conflictos multiculturales de la globalización* (1995) and *La globalización imaginada* (1999). In *Consumidores y ciudadanos*, García Canclini attempts to theorise what it means to be a citizen-consumer in globalised, multicultural cities within national boundaries. In particular, how daily life and the public sphere have been transformed by the communication media, such that the individual is saturated daily by conflicting images and ideological messages and the boundaries between different manifestations of culture are increasingly blurred. García Canclini wants to investigate how, given that contemporary societies are unrepentantly consumerist, this consumerism might be channelled into effective citizenship, that is, how civil society might co-exist and thrive by accommodating to a more moderate and socially responsible consumerism. These concerns overlap with the notion of global civil society as an adjunct or alternative to a restricted or weak national civil society. Like Jesús Martín-Barbero, García Canclini wishes to exploit affirmative possibilities that the mass media have opened up for a "democratization of culture" in a more multicultural and dispersed global public sphere.

George Yúdice subsequently took up this discussion in a special issue of *Social Text* (1995), in which he attempted to combine insights from *Utopia Unarmed* (1993), Jorge Castañeda's controversial ideas for rethinking political economy in Latin America, with García Canclini's more culturalist focus. As an antidote to the weakening of the state vis-à-vis globalisation and neo-liberalism, Castañeda has proposed a Latin American "regional federation" along economic and environmental lines (311). He sees this as an "intermediate solution between a largely unsustainable status quo and a highly harmful progression toward the dissolution of [national] sovereignties" (313). But even though Castañeda attends to the political aspects of such an integration, according to Yúdice, he leaves out the "important dimension [...] of regional cultural integration, which would include the arts, the media, and their relationship (most significantly through consumption) to economic and political factors" ("Civil Society" 18). This cultural factor is the aspect of García Canclini's like-minded proposal that Yúdice sees as essential to such ideas. He summarises García Canclini's regional-federalist proposals as:

> policies to create a Latin American media space; the creation of book, magazine, film, TV, and video common markets in the region; setting quotas of 50 percent Latin American production and distribution in movie

theaters, video outlets, radio broadcasts, television programming [...] the regulation of foreign capital and policies to strengthen Latin American economies; the development of citizenship by giving greater attention to politics of recognition in keeping with a democratic multiculturality. (19)

But the idea of a regional economic-cultural federation, while admirable in its intent, might prove more than a little difficult to establish. Except for some Islamic and African countries, where extreme poverty and lack of infrastructure literally prevent these countries plugging into the global media on a mass scale, national governments world-wide seem incapable of effectively legislating, controlling or shaping cultural responses to global culture and media industries. Strict censorship and national control of media space would appear to be the only solution. But internally, this would be vigorously opposed by citizens as fundamentally un-democratic, and externally it would be resisted by international financial institutions and the dominant world economies. The latter are particularly adept at punishing "renegade" nations that attempt to impose tariff restrictions and state control over flows of information, capital and goods, cultural or otherwise, within globalisation. Furthermore, and as Alberto Moreiras points out, these kinds of projects are still "elements of statist cultural politics" and "excessively timid reformist attempts" with little to prevent them from "being eventually swallowed by global integration and made radically indistinguishable form neoliberal structural compensation" (66).

Subaltern/Postcolonial Studies

Like cultural studies, subaltern studies share a sense of the need to go beyond both the national framework and its homogenising narratives, especially as these are propagated through print culture, and the need to take cognisance of the overwhelming importance of the global mass media in shaping the social and cultural imaginary. But where Latin American subaltern studies marks an initial departure from the style of cultural studies practiced by García Canclini is in the centrality of the notion of the "subaltern", which Gareth Williams regards as a "privileged category and critical perspective from which to grapple with the complexities of current cultural and political configurations in Latin America" (2). The notion of the "people" has long been considered too vague as it occludes class, racial and ethnic tensions within the category. So too the "popular", which has always been uncomfortably linked by association with the discredited projects of authoritarian populism in the twentieth century (most typically Peronism). On the other hand, Gramsci's notion of the "subaltern", as a general condition of subordination, which is equally valid for class, caste, gender, "race", sexuality and so forth, captures more fully the dominant/subordinate binary which the Latin American Subaltern Studies Group believes animates political, cultural and economic struggles.[3]

Furthermore, the concept can be utilized, as it was by Gramsci, to theorise a new hegemonic power bloc – the "national-popular" – in which radical intellectuals and the subaltern unite to forge an anti-bourgeois nation-state.

In their "Founding Statement", they view these struggles as now taking place within a context of post-dictatorship, the collapse of revolutionary projects and "the new dynamics created by the effects of the mass media and transnational economic arrangements [... which] call for new ways of thinking and acting politically" (135–36). Their project would come to involve a study of those cultural forms that are outside the centripetal forces of the bourgeois national state and outside academically sanctioned "Latin American literature" which, in part, underpins the formation of its dominant classes. Thus the importance to the subalternists of *testimonio* in the 1980s as a counter-hegemonic literary genre, one deemed capable of giving expression on the cultural level to a national-popular power bloc. So too the importance, for John Beverley, of the conjunction between oral culture and mass media: "Populations formerly immersed in the primarily oral, iconographic world of rural popular culture can pass [...] directly from that culture to the culture of the media [...] without going through print culture" (*Subalternity* 42–3).

The turn away from canonical literature, whether progressive or not, was occasioned, Beverley believes, by the publication of Ángel Rama's *La ciudad letrada* (1984), which Beverley regards as Rama's own chastened reappraisal of his earlier enthusiasm for "narrative transculturation", a theory which in effect re-inscribes and defuses subaltern difference in a sublation of popular resistance into an imagined social-democratic resolution of racial, cultural and class tensions, led no doubt by Left literary-modernists:

> Latin American literature not only served those nation-states by producing allegorical "foundational fictions", however; literature was also an ideological practice that interpellated the colonial and Creole elites that engendered and ran these states, a form of self-definition and self-legitimization that equated the capacity to write and understand literature with the right to exercise state power. (*Subalternity* 10)

In this process, Latin American literary intellectuals equate with what Gramsci called traditional intellectuals: "lettered intellectuals with a cosmopolitan and universalizing worldview – in Latin America, Spanish *letrados*" (*Subalternity* 12). This is the essence of Beverley's rejection of "neo-Arielism" (the term is his), which he uses to describe the current position of the Uruguayan critics, Mabel Moraña and Hugo Achugar, as well as that of the Argentinian literary and cultural critic, Beatriz Sarlo.

Subaltern studies appear to have undergone two key transformations in recent times. Firstly, the notion of the "national-popular" within revolutionary nationalism has foundered in recent times, due in part to the internal contradictions in the national form itself – the problem of state centralism and its homogenising tendencies, ignoring unresolved linguistic, ethnic, racial, and gender differences – and externally under the disaggregating pressures of neoliberal globalisation. As Gareth Williams sees it: "through increasing transnationalization we are living the historical 'other side' of the national popular; the national-popular in its state of exhaustion and redistribution across regional and national frontiers" (7–8). The second transformation is related to the perceived need to problematise the attempt to represent the subaltern from the academy, which, according to Beverley, becomes an unwitting re-inscription of dominant/subordinate relationships, "compatible with the prolongation of inequalities of class, gender, ethnicity that rule our societies", in effect a form of "postmodern *costumbrismo*", thus the need for a "critique of academic reason" ("Postscriptum" 507). There is an important difference, he believes, between merely adjusting one's knowledge in the academy to the contemporary reality of neoliberal hegemony in a context of collapsed emancipatory left-wing projects (Beverley regards García-Canclini's cultural studies work as just such an instance of this practice), and actively seeking to bring about fundamental change. What is at issue is subaltern agency. Beverley interprets Bhabha's theory of hybridity as offering the "colonial or subaltern subject [the possibility to] 'translate' and 'undo' the binaries imposed by the colonial project itself" (*Subalternity* 16). But this too quickly collapses the radical alterity between the subaltern and the elites in terms of unresolved dominant/subordinate relationships, limiting subaltern resistance, Beverley believes, to a struggle on the terrain of identity politics through the medium of popular or mass culture (16–17). It is interesting in this respect to see in Beverley's complaint a parallel criticism to that directed against Hall earlier in this article for taking British cultural studies in the direction of a sociology of image studies.

The ideas and critiques developed in Latin American subaltern studies are provocative, even if they over-state the case for the necessary imbrication of written literature in domination (a little too mechanistic and too Althusserian in the notion of ideological over-determination). Furthermore, in the introduction to the English version of García Canclini's *Consumers and Citizens*, George Yúdice mounts a spirited defence against what he regards as Beverley's willful misreading of García Canclini's work as a form of self-entrapment within neoliberal market logics by positing consumption as a ground for thinking cultural politics. As one of García Canclini's most important interlocutors, George Yúdice observed several years back that "societies may have reached a historical threshold in which it is no longer possible to think such ideals as citizenship and democracy in the absence of consumption" ("Civil Society" 20). And it is in this sense of there being no outside to neoliberal globalisation that he sees the subalternist project itself as deeply flawed: "Subalternists put a premium on colonial history and have little to say about the engagement of subalterns with media and consumption [... which] render them ineffective as means of empowerment" ("From Hybridity" xxxii). Consequently, the Latin

American Subaltern Studies group has followed the South Asian group in resorting to a conception of negativity (refusal) to counter global modernity. But subalternists, Yúdice declares, paradoxically perform their own erasure of agency by relegating subaltern agency to a labour of negation, negating in the process their own claims for the "pivotal position of the subaltern [...] in the creation of a new historical bloc", with the result that:

> there are, in fact, no "actors" in subalternity. Instead there is the will to refusal [...] Like the will to power, it is a "self-consuming concept" [the term is Beverley's]. The question remains: what can a self-consuming concept offer politics and the "outside" of institutionality? [...] while well-intentioned and properly utopian, [this strategy] seems quite voluntarist, particularly for an academic whose involvement with subalterns is largely textual. (xxxii–iii)

Beverley's work brings sharply into focus both the affinities and the crucial differences between subaltern studies and *estudios culturales*. Both approaches, however, are criticised by *crítica cultural* (cultural critique), to which we now turn.

Cultural Critique

García Canclini, Martín-Barbero, indeed Yúdice (though perhaps much less optimistically than these two theorists) are at one end of the two poles that Gabriela Nouzeilles identifies in Latin American cultural studies:

> The first group corresponds to those who, even though they acknowledge the risks of complicity with the market, regard transnationalization as an opportunity to question both the national state and the totalitarian strategies of the traditional left [...] The exaltation of micropolitics is often accompanied by reliance on the affirmative potential of resistance and creative appropriation of elements coming from the mass media and the all-pervasive culture of consumption. (291)

The other end of this Leftist "political postmodern" is occupied by those who still find continuing relevance in the "lettered city", those who, in the words of Abril Trigo, still cling to "the integrating capabilities of national literatures and art" (75). The most prominent among this group are Mabel Moraña, Hugo Achugar and Beatriz Sarlo. Nelly Richard, while likewise championing the redemptive possibilities of art and literature, practices what she terms "Cultural Critique", which has a strongly anarchist, vanguardist and anti-statist orientation, centred on "writing" as theorised by poststructuralist critics such as Derrida, Kristeva, Barthes and Deleuze: the potential for linguistic interruption as political redemption. Richard shares many of the concerns of both cultural studies and subalternist critiques, especially in the problematisation of academic, theoretical discourse (*Residuos* 142). Richard attempts to differentiate cultural critique from cultural studies via an appeal to different *loci* of enunciation:

cultural critique *from* Latin America by Latin Americans versus academic cultural studies from the United States which speak *about* Latin America, the latter regarded as a form of "Latin-Americanism" and all this implies regarding the history of area studies and the theoretical domination of the North over the South ("Intersectando" 345–6). The opposition breaks down, of course, since García Canclini, one of the emblematic practitioners of cultural studies, is an Argentinian working in Mexico. The point Richard wishes to make, however, is about the imperative to theorise the institutional location from which one speaks and which necessarily (in her opinion) conditions the ideological valency of one's utterances.

While Richard's thinking is anti-statist, Sarlo, Moraña and Achugar still seem fundamentally attached to nationalist models and the role of the lettered intellectual in state formation. Nevertheless, all appear united in their mutual suspicion towards the claims of leftist cultural discourses emanating from the US academy. In addition, they are all equally oriented towards modernist and vanguardist literature, the "specificity of the literary-aesthetic" and its redemptive possibilities, as Richard puts it (*Residuos* 150). Sarlo is also worried by what she regards as the levelling tendencies of cultural studies in regard to "the question of aesthetic values, of the specific qualities of the literary text" (Sarlo 115). The difference between cultural studies and cultural critique could therefore be said to revolve around the respective claims of a cultural studies oriented towards a sociological critique of the popular and mass media versus an aestheticist cultural critique of the modernist and avant-garde canon: "Cultural critique construes its locus from 'aesthetic materiality' [...] That is, it concerns the way in which drives and instincts, desire, pleasure and *jouissance* materialize in a text through the act of writing" (Sarto 236).

One of the key differences between subaltern studies and the type of cultural critique practiced by Richard and Sarlo lies in the conception of the role of aesthetic modernism and its "goals of estrangement and defamiliarization" (Beverley, *Subalternity* 106). These goals were posited within a notion of an at least partially established autonomous aesthetic sphere, like that theorized within modernity by Habermas. The question is, therefore, to what degree such autonomy still exists and thus what redemptive possibilities still remain in the aesthetic within the reality of contemporary globalisation in which economy and culture, public and private, "have been pried open to each other" (Yúdice, "Privatization" 26)? For Sarlo and Richard, the "specificity of the literary-aesthetic" seems to function in much the same way as it did for Adorno: a zone of creativity and imagination, its power residing in its "autonomy" and non-instrumentality ("negativity"). The crucial question then becomes that of the nature of the aesthetic: how do we define the aesthetic and what is the value of the (radical) aesthetic? For it would seem that from this account, the aesthetic is defined functionally as a negativity to domination, which amounts to an unworkable and vague definition. Furthermore, in purely political terms, that which adopts a stance of willed negativity and non-utilitarianism hardly represents a threat to dominant power structures and invites essentially the same criticism directed above by Yúdice at subaltern studies: reducing subalternism to a labour of refusal tends to negates its agency. It would seem then that works regarded as aesthetically radical function more as a consolation for their producers and interested receivers than as edifying examples for the downtrodden. This returns us to the unresolved problem of how to bridge the gap between intellectual radicalism and the exploited "masses".

According to Julio Ramos, for both Sarlo and Richard, the privileging of aesthetic negativity and its "capacity to present alternative worlds to the instrumental logic of the market and neo-liberal middle ground", occurs within "post-dictatorial contexts and democracies in transition [in which they] assign a certain privilege to aesthetic authority in the ongoing debate on democracy" (247). But as the nation-state increasingly fractures under the dual impact of division from below (the unfulfilled promise of two hundred years of independence) and from above by globalisation, "the current crisis felt in cultural institutions (and the republican pedagogical apparatus) tends to cancel both the intellectual's representative role and the privilege granted to the cultural-aesthetic project, as two forms of authority central to the interpretation of subjects as citizens" (Ramos 248).

I would like to complete this unavoidably selective and admittedly reductive view of Latin American cultural studies by briefly mentioning Walter Mignolo's valuable work on "colonial difference", but also his entrapment in a specious politics of location. In *The Darker Side of the Renaissance* (1995) and more recently *Local Histories/Global Designs: Coloniality, Subaltern Knowledges, and Border Thinking* (2000), Mignolo, at one stage also a member of the Latin American Subaltern Studies Group, is keen to problematise what he regards as the self-validating narrative of European modernity, which obscures the fact that its unfolding was based on coloniality: the plundering of "New World" wealth and the concomitant European act of self-definition as "civilisation" through positing the colonial other as "savage". To counter this historical tendency, Mignolo posits "colonial difference" and "border thinking" in which the "restitution of subaltern knowledge is taking place" and where "colonial difference is the space [...] in which global designs have to be adapted, adopted, rejected, integrated, or ignored" (*Local Histories* ix).

In an earlier article in which he responds to Peter Hulme's criticism of his privileging an epistemology of location, Mignolo elaborates on what he regards as the dilemma of historical thinking, even in such a perceptive subaltern historian as Dipesh Chakrabarty: "The basis of [the] 'Chakrabarty dilemma' is that writing subaltern 'histories' means to remain in an epistemically subaltern position in the domain of cultures of scholarship. This is because one of the invisible places in which the coloniality of power operates is the domain of epistemology" ("I Am" 241). In other words, the institutional location of much history writing already compromises what can be said by the very methodological and philosophical assumptions of "professional" historiography. Commenting on the exclusion of the voice of the indigene in Gordon Brotherston's discussion of Amerindian knowledge of a system of writing, Mignolo declares:

> Amerindians themselves have nothing to say, as they have not been invited to participate in a debate in which they themselves are objects of consideration. That is the epistemic colonial difference from whence emerged Amerindians in the sixteenth century, Chicano/as in the US today, and white, mestizo, and immigrant Creole intellectuals like Kusch, Dussel, and myself. "Voices from the margins" are voices from and dealing with the colonial epistemic difference. (241)

In *Local Histories/Global Designs*, he elaborates on this colonial difference from the point of view of a sensual, lived experience related to territory: "the sensibilities of geohistorical locations have to do with a sense of territoriality [...] and include language, food, smells, landscape, climate, and all the basic signs that link the body to one or several places" (191).

No doubt there is a degree of truth to this sort of claim, but *how* each person experiences those sensibilities will be crucially related to socio-economic position. Mignolo unfortunately collapses the distance between Amerindians and "white, mestizo, and immigrant Creole intellectuals like Kusch, Dussel" and himself, seemingly oblivious to the obvious objection that there is also a world of class, status and ethnic differences between the lettered intellectual able to participate in, indeed make a living from, engaging in Euro-Latin American cultural debates, and the Amerindians. Here the politics of location is reduced to an abstract macro-geo-cultural category – "Latin America" – now reconstituted, not as the now largely discredited US area studies, but as the site of "colonial difference", in which the privileged interlocutors (once more) are the lettered Creole intelligentsia. There is more than a ring of truth therefore to Peter Hulme's remark that "birth certificates matter more here than intellectual credentials" (225). Mignolo rebels against what he regards as the subordination of Latin American intellectuals vis-à-vis metropolitan centres of learning, but though such one-way traffic of knowledge does exist, it may matter much less in relation to the difference lived by the subordinate classes in the postcolonial, peripheral nation than that which is experienced by the postcolonial national intelligentsia itself.

Conclusion

A set of defining characteristics of modern cultural studies was outlined above. One definition seeks to posit cultural studies as the study of both popular and "elite" cultural products and processes. The word "elite" is ironic here to draw attention to the (mistaken) habit of regarding elite literature as a class-based literature: elitism does not inhere in the text (which is not to deny the possibility of "elite" content in some texts), but is constructed as elite via its reception and classification by a valuing community concerned with canon-formation. Williams's own work transgressed the boundaries between elite and popular cultures. But this transgression is also implied in, for example, Easthope's understanding of "literary study" as "increasingly indistinguishable from cultural studies" (65), and in Tony Bennett's sense of cultural studies as fundamentally concerned with "relations of culture and power" (53). All cultural practices provide a window onto sociality and history and the power structures that traverse them.

Though many aspects of so-called Latin American cultural studies have developed independently of trends within British cultural studies, the most promising developments of both traditions share some essential characteristics: they are multi- or trans-disciplinary; address issues of culture and power; and they are culturally materialist, that is, contextually and historically grounded in political economy. But the differences are important too. Where Latin American cultural studies differ and where British and US cultural studies can profit from their work, is in the increased emphasis on the problematic relationship between intellectuals and the subaltern and thus the issue of the politics of enunciation. Latin American cultural studies has been more concerned with the role of the intellectual in relation to the oppressed about whom and for whom they propose to speak, and more than anything else, this concern appears to have two main causes, respectively "external" and "internal". Firstly, the uneasiness felt by those who use European or North American theories to investigate Latin American cultural reality and the related problem of intellectual colonisation; and secondly, the profound change in attitude effected by Ángel Rama's *La ciudad letrada*: the imbrication of lettered culture with institutional (state) power structures. While the second issue was addressed in Anglo-American cultural theory through Foucault's more global concept of "governmentality", the notion of the specific versus the universal intellectual still failed to address adequately the problematic relationship between intellectuals and the downtrodden and does not seem to have been a problem for Anglo-North American cultural theorists. One searches in vain in the work of Raymond Williams or Stuart Hall, for instance, for a sustained reflection on the legitimacy of the intellectual speaking for the underclasses.

Cultural studies in Latin America are as diverse as the objective social and cultural situations in which they are generated and the presence of large non-European, indigenous populations has historically inflected cultural thought in Latin America since colonisation over 500 years ago. The issue of the non-European other has only become a pressing issue in Britain in relatively recent times, since the post-World War II migration of non-white colonial subjects into the heart of empire. Thus a tradition largely absent from Euro-North American theorising, except in the reductive discourses of traditional anthropology, has been the theorising in Latin America of cultural mixing in the form of *mestizaje*, *raza cósmica*, *transculturación*, *heterogeneidad*, *hibridez*, and so forth. Though there are problems with each designation and their attempts to suture over the continuing class, ethnic and racial divisions within Latin American societies, the tradition is largely free of the racist overtones and the negative and power-laden connotations inherent in such English terms as "miscegenation", "acculturation" and "assimilation".

By extension, the strong presence in Latin America of "popular culture", understood not merely as mass or urban culture, as in Western industrialised countries, but also the auratic, or semi-auratic, modes of being of indigenous cultures, brings a whole set of different issues to Latin American cultural studies (the argument about so-called co-existing modes of production and world views). In Latin America, popular culture has always meant much more than massification or mere entertainment for the popular classes; it has also been an integral and integrating expression of deeper community values, values that have not been provided by the state, which historically has been formed before civil society and which has reduced modernisation to a mainly economic affair. Until recent times, much popular cultural expression has been decidedly pre-modern in its outlook and in relation to the worldviews that underpin its processes. For this reason, cultural critics both inside and outside Latin America must work subtly in analysing cultural production, since there is no such thing as Latin American culture in the singular, popular or otherwise. A markedly different situation obtains in the more developed world where industrialisation, urbanism, secularism and high levels of mass education have removed popular cultural expression (for instance, music, handicrafts, and festivals) from its functional unity with religion and daily life. Art, like politics, education, economy, science, in fact all aspects of modern society, has been functionally differentiated into separate spheres and this has implications for alienation and reification. But in Latin America, while many large cities mimic the political, economic, social and cultural structures of the European and North American nation-states, the cultures of many non-urban areas, including indigenous culture, still move to the rhythms of rural life and within the bonds of communal ideals. Indeed, vestiges of pre-modern practices can still be found even in large cities, where *campesino* classes continually flow into the cities seeking work or refuge from regional violence (most notably in Peru, Mexico, Colombia and Central America). In Mexico, Colombia, the Andean countries, Central America, and parts of Brazil, there is thus a co-existence of different modes of production, different temporalities, different cosmogonies, and these have profound implications for cultural processes and analyses thereof.

What we need to do, I would like to suggest, is to continue to seek positive connections to see what can be critically generated by placing both versions of cultural studies outlined above in productive juxtaposition so as to contribute towards some sort of collective, transnational framework for cultural studies, but one which acknowledges both non-metropolitan difference as well as the contributions made by peripheral "barbarian" theorists, and this often in difficult conditions.[4] But in turn these theorists need to disabuse themselves of essentialism, trying to bracket homegrown cultural theorists off from "outside" influences or claiming some dubious "authenticity" over and against their opposite number in non-Latin American countries, as if there were some uncontaminated theoretical space. Furthermore, academics and intellectuals need to be a lot more modest about what they think they can achieve by prosecuting a largely textualist politics from inside the academy:

> If it is true that intellectuals have championed the subaltern, it is also true that they have monopolized the place that others could have created. That space has been reclaimed in the last two decades [...] by the social movements, especially the base movements. And with this "explosion of the base", when civil society emerges, the role of the intellectual is diminished. These become fellow travelers, chroniclers or recorders of *testimonios* like Carlos Monsiváis and Elena Poniatowska who, let it be said, foreground the knowledge of the popular sectors. Now there is no need for prophetic, redemptive or illuminating knowledge from the type of writer like Neruda or Fuentes. (Yúdice "Postmodernidad")

Thus academics need to decide if their practice has political impact or, if not, if it is just a form of prestige or cultural capital. There is nothing wrong with literary and cultural theorists working within academia and espousing progressive politics: they just need to be content with much more modest outcomes for what they do. And many of the current poisonous debates among Latin American literary and cultural critics over the "authenticity" of their respective theoretical positions, methodologies and *loci* of enunciation have to do precisely with a deep anxiety about both their role and effectiveness (or lack thereof) in a context of collapsing Leftist narratives, and perhaps the suspicion that their relentless textualism has no direct impact on political events (the question of audience). But if they insist on wringing their hands in relation to their legitimacy as interlocutors of, or spokespersons for, the oppressed, then the most satisfying kind of appeasement of guilt can be obtained by getting involved with political movements and organisations outside academia as an antidote to their academicism. After all, the real frontline in contemporary struggles against a capitalism as voracious as any in history can be found in the new social movements, in trade union activity, in street protests, and so forth.

Cultural studies works at the interface between "system" and "life-world". In Habermas, the former refers to the sphere of the economy and the state, money and power, which functions through the logic of instrumental reason; the latter to the world of everyday experience, social discourse and cultural values, science, politics and art. This returns us to the problem of legitimation. Jürgen

Habermas has claimed that states cannot be self-legitimating because of their inherent rationality, as Max Weber had supposed; rather their validity must flow from their moral and political dimensions, that is, their ability to guarantee and reflect the will of all people. But the "will of the people" can never be assumed nor can it be simply guaranteed by the Habermasian bourgeois public sphere (and its lettered intellectuals), even less by the performance of formal democracy: it must also flow from cultural orientation, custom and lived experience. For Williams's cultural materialism, the concretely experiential has remained stubbornly relevant, not so much as the antithesis of, but as the complement to, abstract reason. As Eagleton observes:

> Williams's subtle sense of the complex mediations between such necessarily universal formations as social class, and the lived particularities of place, region, Nature, the body, contrasts tellingly with Habermas's universalist rationalism. Williams's social theory refuses at once a "bad" universalism and what he terms a "militant particularism". (409)

Perhaps Williams's work is the most reliable bridge between British and Latin American cultural criticism, which, in spite of important differences among its practitioners and their theories, perform analogous materialist engagements with history and its cultural processes. This is their ongoing promise, but only if they can manage to steer a path between Williams's double refusal.

Works cited

Achugar, Hugo. "Leones, cazadores e historiadores: a propósito de las políticas de la memoria y del conocimiento." *Revista Iberoamericana* 180 (1997): 379–87.

Arnold, Mathew. *Culture and Anarchy.* Ed. J. D. Wilson. Cambridge: Cambridge University Press, 1966.

Bauman, Zigmunt. *Legislators and Interpreters: On Modernity, Post-modernity and Intellectuals.* Cambridge: Polity Press, 1987.

Bello, Andrés. *Silvas americanas y otros poemas.* Barcelona: Ramón Sopena, 1978.

Bennett, Tony. *Culture: A Reformer's Science.* London: Sage, 1998.

Beverley, John. *Subalternity and Representation: Arguments in Cultural Theory.* Durham: Duke University Press, 1999.

——. "Postscriptum." *Nuevas perspectivas desde/sobre América latina: el desafío de los estudios culturales.* Ed. Mabel Moraña. Santiago: Cuarto Propio, 2000. 499–508.

Bolívar, Simón. *Carta de Jamaica.* Caracas: Ministerio de Educación, 1965.

Browitt, Jeff. "After the Fall: J. L. Borges and Romantic Individualism." *Anales* 3.2 (1994): 59–74.

——. "*Modernismo* and the Genesis of the Autonomous Literary Field in Latin America." *Pierre Bourdieu and the Field of Cultural Production.* Ed. Jeff Browitt. Newark: Monash Romance Studies / University of Delaware Press, (in press).

Castañeda, Carlos. *Utopia Unarmed: The Latin American Left after the Cold War.* New York: Knopf, 1993.

Eagleton. Terry. *The Ideology of the Aesthetic.* Oxford: Basil Blackwell, 1990.

Easthope, Anthony. *Literary into Cultural Studies.* London: Routledge, 1991.

García Canclini, Nestor. *Culturas híbridas: estrategias para entrar y salir de la modernidad.* México, D. F.: Grijalbo, 1989.
——.*Consumidores y ciudadanos: conflictos multiculturales de la globalización.* México, D. F.: Grijalbo, 1995.
——. *Consumers and Citizens: Globalization and Multicultural Conflicts.* Trans. and intro. by George Yúdice. Minneapolis: University of Minnesota Press, 2001.
——. *La globalización imaginada.* Buenos Aires: Paidós, 1999.
Gramsci, Antonio. *Selections from Prison Notebooks.* Trans. Q. Hoare and G. Nowell Smith. London: Lawrence and Wishart, 1971.
Hall, Stuart. "Cultural Studies: Two Paradigms." *Media, Culture and Society* 2.1 (1980): 57–72.
——."For Allon White: Metaphors of Transformation." *Stuart Hall: Critical Dialogues in Cultural Studies.* Eds. David. Morley and K. Chen. London: Routledge, 1996
Hall, Stuart and T. Jefferson, eds. *Resistance through Rituals: Youth Subcultures in Post-War Britain.* London: Hutchinson, 1976.
Hall, Stuart and Paddy Whannel. *The Popular Arts.* London: Hutchinson, 1964.
Higgins, John. *Raymond Williams: Literature, Marxism and Cultural Materialism.* London: Routledge, 1999.
Hoggart, Richard. *The Uses of Literacy.* Harmondsworth: Penguin, 1958.
Hulme, Peter. "Voice from the Margins? Walter Mignolo's *The Darker Side of the Renaissance.*" *Journal of Latin American Cultural Studies,* 8.2 (1999): 219–33.
Latin American Subaltern Studies Group. "Founding Statement." *The Postmodern Debate in Latin America.* Eds. John Beverley, José Oviedo, and Michael Aronna. Durham: Duke University Press, 1995.
Mariátegui, José Carlos. *Siete ensayos de interpretación de la realidad peruana.* Lima: Amauta, 1928.
Martín-Barbero, Jesús. *De los medios a las mediaciones. Comunicación, cultura y hegemonía.* Gili, México, 1987.
——. "Interview." *Journal of Latin American Cultural Studies* 10.2 (2001): 223–30.
Mignolo, Walter. "I Am Where I Think: Epistemology and the Colonial Difference." *Journal of Latin American Cultural Studies* 8.2 (1999): 235–45.
——. *The Darker Side of the Renaissance: Literacy, Territoriality and Colonialization.* Ann Arbor: University of Michigan Press, 1995.
——. *Local Histories/Global Designs: Coloniality, Subaltern Knowledges, and Border Thinking,* Princeton: Princeton University Press, 2000.
Milner, Andrew and Jeff Browitt. *Contemporary Cultural Theory.* London / New York: Routledge, 2002.
Moraña, Mabel. "El boom del subalterno." *Revista de Crítica Cultural* 14 (1997): 48–53.
Moreiras, Alberto. *The Exhaustion of Difference.* Durham: Duke University Press, 2001.
Nouzeilles, Gabriela. "Apocalyptic Visions: National Tales and Cultural Analysis in a Global Argentina." *Journal of Latin American Cultural Studies* 10.3 (2001): 291–301.
Ortiz, Fernando. *Contrapunteo del tabaco y el azúcar.* La Habana: Montero, 1940.
Peck, Janice. "Itinerary of a Thought: Stuart Hall, Cultural Studies, and the Unresolved Problem of the Relation of Culture to 'Not Culture.'" *Cultural Critique* 48 (2001): 200–49.
Rama, Ángel. *La ciudad letrada.* Hanover: Ediciones del Norte, 1984.
Ramos, Julio. "Hemispheric Domains: 1898 and the Origins of Latin Americanism." *Journal of Latin American Cultural Studies* 10.3 (2001): 237–51.

Richard, Nelly. "Intersectando Latinoamérica con el Latinoamericanismo: discurso académico y crítica cultural." *Revista Iberoamericana* 180 (1997): 345–61.

——. *Residuos y metáforas. Ensayos de crítica cultural sobre el Chile de la transición.* Santiago: Cuarto Propio, 1998.

Sarlo, Beatriz. "Cultural Studies and Literary Criticism at the Crossroads of Values." *Journal of Latin American Cultural Studies* 8.1 (1999): 115–24.

Sarmiento, Domingo Faustino. *Facundo: civilización y barbarie*, Madrid: Alianza, 1970.

Sarto, Ana del. "Cultural Critique in Latin America or Latin-American Cultural Studies?" *Journal of Latin American Cultural Studies* 9.3 (2000): 235–47.

Thompson, Edward P. *The Making of the English Working Class.* London: Victor Gollancz, 1963.

Trigo, Abril. "Why Do I Do Cultural Studies?" *Journal of Latin American Cultural Studies* 9.1 (2000): 73–93.

Williams, Gareth. *The Other Side of the Popular*, Durham: Duke University Press, 2002.

Williams, Raymond. *Communications.* Harmondsworth: Penguin, 1962.

——. *Culture and Society 1780–1950.* Harmondsworth: Penguin, 1963.

——. *The Long Revolution.* Harmondsworth: Penguin, 1965.

——. *Marxism and Literature.* Oxford: Oxford University Press, 1977.

——. *Problems in Materialism and Culture: Selected Essays.* London: New Left Books, 1980.

——. *Television: Technology and Cultural Form.* Glasgow: Fontana, 1974.

Yúdice, George. "Civil Society, Consumption, and Governmentality in an Age of Global Restructuring: An Introduction." *Social Text* 45 (1995): 1–25.

——. "The Privatization of Culture." *Social Text* 59 (1999): 17–34.

——. "From Hybridity to Policy: For a Purposeful Cultural Studies." *Consumers and Citizens: Globalization and Multicultural Conflicts.* Nestor García Canclini. Trans. and intro. George Yúdice, Minneapolis: University of Minnesota Press, 2001. ix–xxxviii.

——. "Postmodernidad y valores."<http://www.nyu.edu/projects/IACSN/valores.htm>

Notes

[1] The direct reference for these debates is a series of running skirmishes between the members of the now defunct Latin American Subaltern Studies Group and other proponents of cultural studies who go under the rubric of *crítica cultural* and *estudios culturales*. John Beverely has been the most articulate and prominent subalternist, along with Patricia Seed and Ileana Rodríguez. Their critics have variously been Román de la Campa, Mabel Moraña, Hugo Achugar, Beatriz Sarlo, Nelly Richard, Doris Sommer, Walter Mignolo and George Yúdice. Two of the strongest criticisms of subaltern studies, and by extension North American and outside influences, have been mounted by Moraña and Achugar. According to Moraña, subaltern studies perpetuates metropolitan/peripheral relations by keeping Latin America "in the place of the other, a pretheoretical, marginal, calibanesque site in relation to metropolitan discourse" (Moraña 50); for Achugar, "[L]a construcción que se propone de América Latina, dentro del marco teórico de los llamados estudios postcoloniales, parecería apuntar a que el lugar desde donde se habla no es o no debería ser el de la nación sino el del pasado colonial [...] el de la agenda de la academia norteamericana que está localizada en la historia de su sociedad civil" (381).

[2] This is a similar anxiety to that which I have tried to highlight in relation to Jorge Luis Borges (Browitt, "After").

[3] I have chosen to concentrate exclusively on Beverley's work in subaltern studies as he

has been by far its most prominent and articulate spokesperson. The Subaltern Studies Group nevertheless included several other prominent Latin Americanists, including, among others, Ileana Rodríguez and Patricia Seed.

[4] Thus Maritza López de la Roche: "As regards comparisons with the North Americn academy, what should not be lost from sight is the radical inequality of the conditions of production of knowledge of those of us who work in the universities or research centres in Latin American countries, perhaps with the exception of a few institutions in Brazil and Mexico" (personal communication with the author).

Imperial Myopia:
British Visions of Argentina

Kevin Foster

In the closing days of the Falklands War, as a regular flow of photographs and footage of the conflict finally began to arrive in the UK, the completeness of Britain's triumph was enforced and widely advertised through a series of iconic images which focused on the abjectness of Argentina's defeat. Three images in particular were widely distributed at the time of the conflict, and have since appeared in a broad range of histories, memoirs and other accounts of the war, three images which, taken together, offer a concise British narrative of Argentina's defeat and despair. The first of these depicts an unshaven Captain Alfredo Astiz, Argentine military commander of Isla San Pedro or South Georgia, better known perhaps as "*el rubio*", the Angel of Death or the Butcher of Cordoba, for his enthusiastic participation in the rounding up, torture and disappearance of Argentine and foreign nationals during the dirty war, signing the document surrendering the Argentine garrison on South Georgia aboard the British Antarctic survey vessel, *Endurance* (Fig. 1). The second, and there are many versions of this, portrays lines of ragged conscripts, sodden, smoke-blackened and demoralised, surrendering a mountain of rifles to British troops (Fig. 2). The third shows furious Argentine civilians rioting in the Plaza de Mayo when news of the surrender of the garrison on the Malvinas was made public – the same square they had packed ten weeks earlier to acclaim the recovery of the islands and the military leaders who had ordered it (Fig. 3).

However, as compelling as these images are, their implied narrative of *la lucha por las Malvinas* is so reductive as to be fundamentally misleading. It is a narrative which says nothing about Argentina's brilliantly executed operation to recover the islands; nothing about the heroism of the air force pilots, or the often staunch resistance put up by Argentine land forces, many of them conscripts; and nothing at all about the many underlying causes of their ultimate defeat – poor training, poor leadership, poor lines of supply. What we see instead is a familiar if dispiriting procession of stereotypical Latinos – cowardly torturers, deflated braggadocios, and mobs of unruly and unpredictable civilians behaving with a customary disregard for private property or decorum. Indeed, what we see in these pictures is less an historical record, however partial, of Argentina's doomed endeavour to recover the islands than the projection of an ongoing and deeply rooted set of western – in this case British – prejudices about Latin America, its peoples, their histories

Figure 1

Figure 2

Figure 3

and cultures. Little wonder, then, that these images say so little about the Argentine experience of the war as they are actually concerned, primarily, with British perceptions of and responses to it.

What do they tell us about these perceptions and responses? The British popular press's reaction to the outbreak and conduct of the conflict was comprised largely of triumphalist cheerleading, neatly summarised in the *Sun*'s most infamous headlines from the war. Alongside the infamous "GOTCHA!" which greeted the sinking of the Argentine cruiser General Belgrano, these included "IT'S WAR!", "WALLOP", "WE'LL SMASH 'EM", "STICK IT UP YOUR JUNTA", and, bumped to the back page on the day the Pope prayed for peace at an open-air mass in Manchester, "HERO BAYONET TROOPS KILL FIFTY" (*Sun*, 1982: 3.5.82; 5.4.82; 27.5.82; 3.4.82; 7.4.82; 14.6.82). The media's full-speed advance on the South Atlantic, all headlines blazing, left little scope, and few column inches for the consideration, even the expression, of some of the genuine anxieties raised by the nation's precipitate commitment to recover the islands: anxieties about the military's preparedness, expertise and equipment, anxieties about the political pitfalls of what seemed to be an anachronistic gesture and the public's willingness to support it, anxieties about the legitimacy of Britain's continuing status as a "world power", the fear that, as Margaret Thatcher put it, "Britain was no longer the nation that had built an Empire and ruled a quarter of the world" (qtd. in Barnett 150). While the British press, with the exception of *The Guardian* and *The Financial Times*, remained conspicuously silent about such concerns, parliamentarians from both sides of the House gave vent to their anger over what had already happened in the South Atlantic and their trepidation over what was yet to come. As the Tory grandee Sir Julian Amery balefully observed in the first Emergency Parliamentary Debate called in response to Argentina's seizure of the islands: "The third naval power in the world and the second in NATO has suffered a humiliating defeat" (Barnett 38). Humiliation, as Patrick Cormack, also from the government benches, noted, not only engendered the determination to redeem the situation and restore the nation's credibility but also excited the fear that this might not be possible, the fear that Britain was not the nation it once was and the anxiety that it might not be able to honour its commitments to its few remaining colonies: "I should think there will be some anxious people in Gibraltar today [...] There will also be anxious people in Hong Kong" (Barnett 39). Indeed, Edward du Cann, wondered if the nation could ever stand up for itself again, if some Darwinian principle hadn't finally caught up with and rolled over it: "For all our alliances and for all the social politenesses which the diplomats so often mistake for trust, in the end in life it is self-reliance and only self-reliance that counts" (Morgan 10).

In this context it is not difficult to see that while the representation of Argentina, its military and its public in these iconic images of the conflict may offer a reductive record of some of its significant events, the primary purpose of these images is to embody and exorcise what the British themselves most feared in the South Atlantic, political humiliation, military collapse, public outrage and social division. Accordingly, from this perspective the Argentines play a subordinate, largely symbolic role in the conflict, in that what Britain is confronting in the South Atlantic is less the Argentine military or the hostility of the elements than itself, its fears about its moral, military and political adequacy in the modern world, long-standing anxieties about the identity and destiny of the nation. The Argentines serve firstly to catalyse and embody these anxieties, and finally to signify their defeat and dispersal.

If this determination to deny the Argentines a substantive role in the fight for the Malvinas was not bad enough, Ian Curteis's mercifully unfilmed television drama, *The Falklands Play* (1987), adds insult to injury by confining the Argentines to an essentially structural role in the conflict, intended, above all else, to enhance the celebration of Britain's moral, military and political superiority. As we see little of either the British or Argentine public in the play, beyond a couple of tellingly framed crowd shots, and nothing at all of the troops engaged in the fight for the islands, the oppositions between the two nations are embodied in and articulated through Curteis's representation of the political protagonists from the opposing sides. While the oppositions between them are stark, they are also entirely predictable in that the leading players from either side are represented not as fully realised, mimetically plausible figures, driven by particular motivations, assisted or hindered by specific strengths or flaws, but as the products and subordinates of a determining plot, mere *acteurs* in a fable of moral antagonism. Accordingly, the primary function of the characters, particularly the Argentines, is semiotic, to organise the elements of the screenplay into a meaningful structure of binary oppositions. The positive pole in this structure is embodied by the British: stout defenders of human rights, democracy and the rule of law, they are presented through a plethora of affirming descriptors: *"vigorous", "immaculately fresh and well-groomed", "tough and firm", "crisp, decisive, irrepressibly cheerful, with a dead straight, twinkly look", "fresh, confident, energetic and suddenly with an indefinable aura of Churchillian relish for the struggle ahead"* (Curteis 56, 114, 130, 110). Even John Nott, the Secretary of State for Defence, whose performance during the campaign was widely criticised, speaks *"with attack and resolve, eyes flashing behind spectacles"* (117). These characterisations determine that the Argentines will be as malignant and incompetent as their opponents are virtuous and efficient. As such, the moral, political and social dysfunctions of the Argentine state, which the screenplay takes pain to detail, its disregard for human rights, the rule of domestic or international law, the standards of political fair play or simple moral decency, merely provide a context for and not an explanation of the junta's incompetence, brutality and malice. Accordingly, its *"most intelligent and liberal"* member, the Air

Force chief, Basilio Lami Dozo, spends the entire screenplay collapsed on the peripheries of the action, *"a crumpled teddy bear of a man"*: insufficiently malicious, he can occupy no meaningful role in the semiotic of moral extremes and so he is simply written out of the screenplay, "disappeared" in the interests of moral hygiene (61).

The source and symbol of the junta's moral otherness is the naval chief Admiral Jorge Anaya: *"slim, vulpine and unsmiling [...] a hard man whose voice betrays no flicker of warmth or humanity"* (61). This is a telling description in that it offers an implicit explanation for Anaya's determination to repossess the Malvinas by force: he does what he is, and what he is is determined by what he is not – British. General Galtieri is less the instigator than the hapless if willing dupe of the malice of others: a *"big, handsome, hard-drinking cavalry officer with hearty, drill-ground manner"*, he is there less to suggest the moral bankruptcy of the Argentine state than to imply the buffoonish incompetence that has, in part, made it possible (61). Always a couple of steps behind the wily Anaya, he lurches through the screenplay in a drink-soaked stupor, swilling whisky from *"huge tumblers"*, stumbling into the swollen furniture, politically and socially far out of his depth (113). Beyond the minimal requirements of plot development, his exchanges with Anaya consistently verge on the risible, as the two men talk merely to reaffirm their place in the overall moral architecture of the play, one a fool, one a villain:

> GALTIERI: Have some popcorn.
>
> ANAYA (*screwing up his face*): How can you eat that filth!
>
> GALTIERI: What's wrong with it? You ought to try some.
> (*He crams it into his mouth washing it down with Glenfiddich. Anaya stares out of the windows at the tree tops*). (62)

These British accounts of the conflict clearly drive home Argentina's final abjection in and over the Falklands War. Instead of acknowledging the ingenuousness of Argentine convictions and the zeal and tenacity with which they pursued them, the British deny them even their own substantiveness, their embodied opposition to the British position and, in a gesture of effortless cultural cannibalism, they ingest and subsume them. They identify the Argentines merely as projections of their own collective uncertainty about the validity of their national self-image and by disappearing the opposition affirm their conquest of the anxieties they embody. From this perspective, it wasn't that the Argentines lost the Falklands War, they never even contested it: the British had been fighting themselves all along.

The nature of the British response to Argentina during the struggle for the Malvinas, its determination to identify it as both the locus and the proxy for its own preoccupations continues a long established pattern of discursive relations between Latin America and Britain, a pattern whose precedents J. H. Elliott identifies in the earliest European responses to the New World.

Surveying a wide array of texts from the late sixteenth century through into the seventeenth century, Elliott observes:

> . . . it is difficult not to be impressed by the strange lacunae and the re-sounding silences in many places where references to the New World could reasonably be expected. How are we to explain the absence of any mention of the New World in so many memoirs and chronicles, including the memoirs of Charles V himself? How are we to explain the continuing determination, right up to the last two or three decades of the sixteenth century, to describe the world as if it were still the world as known to Strabo, Ptolemy and Pomponius Mela? [...]
>
> The reluctance of cosmographers or social philosophers to incorporate into their work the new information made available to them by the discovery of America provides an example of the wider problem arising from the revelation of the New World to the old. Whether it is a question of the geography of America, its flora and fauna, or the nature of its inhabitants, the same kind of pattern seems constantly to recur in the European response. It is as if, at a certain point, the mental shutters came down; as if, with so much to see and absorb and understand, the effort suddenly becomes too much for them, and Europeans retreat to the half-light of their traditional mental world.
>
> There is nothing very novel about the form of this sixteenth century response. Medieval Europe had found it supremely difficult to comprehend and come to terms with the phenomenon of Islam [...] Nor is this a matter for surprise for the attempt of one society to comprehend another inevitably forces it to reappraise itself [... and] This process is bound to be an agonizing one, involving the jettisoning of many traditional preconceptions and inherited ideas. It is hardly surprising, then, if sixteenth-century Europeans either ignored the challenge or baulked at the attempt. There was, after all, an easier way out, neatly epitomized in 1528 by the Spanish humanist, Hernán Pérez de Oliva, when he wrote that Columbus set out on his second voyage "to unite the world and give to those strange lands the form of our own". (13–15)

Elliott's image of sixteenth century Europeans dazzled by the prodigality of the New World, retreating to "the half light of their traditional mental world" provides a key image for the processes determining the English-speaking west's contemporary cultural relations with Latin America. Yet how can one explain the persistence of this perennial ignorance; how is it that where Latin America is concerned the mental shutters remain locked and bolted in the English-speaking west and we are happy to stumble around in the half-light of incomprehension and prejudice? *Ornamentalism* (2001), David Cannadine's recent study of "how the British saw their empire", offers a useful (if unintended) adjunct to Elliott's analysis which may help to explain the persistence of this intellectual half-light through its illustration of how British responses to Latin America were shaped by the precedents and principles drawn from its experience of its overseas colonies.

It is Cannadine's explicit aim in *Ornamentalism* both to draw attention to and correct the approach of British and foreign scholars who had traditionally regarded British imperial history "as if it were completely separate and distinct from the history of the British nation". On the contrary, Cannadine contends, "Britain was very much a part of the empire, just as the rest of the empire was very much part of Britain", the two comprising, in the words of P. D. Morgan, an "entire interactive system", one "vast interconnected world" (*Ornamentalism* xvii). Indeed the empire was, he argued, literally inconceivable in isolation from the metropolitan centre, in that the domestic environment furnished both a model and a means by which the broader populace might conceive of and so understand the empire. What this meant in practical terms for those Britons struggling to "conceive of these diverse colonies and varied populations beyond the seas" was that they began "with what they knew – or what they thought they knew – namely, the social structure of their own home country" (*Ornamentalism* 3–4). And what was it that they (thought they) knew about this structure? Summarising the conclusions of his previous book, *Class in Britain* (1999), Cannadine argues that through the heyday of the empire, from the 1850s to the 1950s:

> Far from seeing themselves as atomized individuals with no rooted sense of identity, or as collective classes coming into being and struggling with each other, or as equal citizens whose modernity engendered an unrivalled sense of progressive superiority, Britons generally conceived of themselves as belonging to an unequal society characterized by a seamless web of layered gradations [...] which extended in a great chain of being from the monarch at the top to the humblest subject at the bottom [...] and it was from that starting point that they contemplated and tried to comprehend the distant realms and diverse society of their empire. (*Ornamentalism* 4)

Consequently, Cannadine affirms, the people's perception of the empire:

> was not exclusively (or even preponderantly) concerned with the creation of "othernesss" on the presumption that the imperial periphery was different from, and inferior to, the imperial metropolis: it was at least as much (perhaps more?) concerned with what has recently been called the "construction of affinities" on the presumption that society on the periphery was the same as, or even on occasions superior to, society in the metropolis. Thus regarded, the British Empire was about the familiar and domestic, as well as the different and the exotic: indeed, it was in large part about the domestication of the exotic – the comprehending and the reordering of the foreign in parallel, analogous, equivalent, resemblant terms. (*Ornamentalism* xix)

Accordingly, one of the central, if unforeseen, functions of the empire, Cannadine asserts, was its provision of a powerful and peculiarly effective "mechanism for the export, projection and analogisation of domestic social structures and social perceptions" (*Ornamentalism* 10).

In spite of the fact that no part of Latin America was ever a formal constituent of the British Empire (with the exception of Belize, British Guyana and, to stretch a point, the Falkland Islands), it seems to me that Cannadine's arguments about British constructions of the empire can offer a useful basis for approaching its discursive relations with Latin America. Indeed, Britain's lack of an imperial presence in Latin America and the mechanism for self-projection that this afforded proved not a bar but a vital stimulus to the export of its domestic vision. If, as the social psychologist Frederick Bartlett points out, "acts of perception are really acts of recall", then what the British saw in Latin America was crucially determined by what they remembered of or had read about equivalent prior experience and the preconceptions they fed (Bartlett 14). The effort to order and understand new experiences, to absorb and evaluate unfamiliar states or situations involves a combination of what cognitive scientists term "bottom-up" and "top-down" processing. Bottom-up processing involves "building up a composite meaning on the basis of our perception of its component parts"; top-down processing, as its name implies, draws on the "expectations, assumptions and prior knowledge" of the interpreter (MacLachlan 70). While regular contact between Britain and its colonies and a healthy traffic in goods and people served to demystify and even suburbanise many of the empire's exoticisms, to convert a raft of top-down assumptions into the embodied evidence of bottom-up observation, ongoing (and repeatedly professed) ignorance about Latin America necessitated a primary – and thereafter habitual – recourse to top-down processes, to prejudice and preconceptions, to the framework of assumptions and expectations they provided within which experience and observation might be ordered and explained. Put simply, where familiarity with the empire served to validate and entrench domestic analogy, continued ignorance of Latin America required it.

This, it should be noted, is not a uniquely British response. Consider the QANTAS advertisement from February 1999 publicising the Australian carrier's newly established direct connections to Buenos Aires: "Let the airline you know show you the land you don't know ... South America" (*The Age* 9) (Fig. 4). The emphasis here is on how domestic forms can provide both emotional lagging and a conceptual framework within which the unknown and threatening might be understood and demystified. QANTAS won't only take you to South America, but as the copy and the photographs of the continent's significant sites demonstrate, they'll also transport your mental luggage, making sure that your expectations and assumptions about South America arrive and remain intact:

> Discover the land of the Andes, the Amazon and the lost cities of the Incas and Aztec. Sprawling pampas, spectacular glaciers and haunting deserts.
>
> This is South America.
>
> And if you're into discovering the brighter side of life – Bienvenido!

Figure 4

> Welcome to the vibrant rhythms of the Lambada, Samba, Rhumba and Mambo. After all this is also the land of the Carnival, Ipanema and Copacabana. (*The Age* 9)

South America, from this advertisement, looks like an eerily depopulated waste, barely marked by the hand of man. Framed by its towering peaks and jungle torrents the land is reduced to its pure, elemental forms – ice, grass, sand; too cold, too hot or just too big. Where there are signs of human habitation the people are either dead or dancing – their cities "lost" or entirely given over to the pleasures of the flesh.

What is most striking about this advertisement, then, is not its reductive representation of Latin America as a cavalcade of tits, tango and torrents, but the extent to which this vision draws on and reproduces Australian constructions of Australia. Efforts to sell Australia as a tourist destination to both foreign and domestic markets have, as Stephen Alomes notes, been framed around a familiar roll call of what he calls "native exotica – flora, fauna and Aborigines" – and sport (175). This vision of Australia as a land of the physical, where nature still holds sway over culture's feeble efforts to leave its mark on the land, translates into the familiar brochure clichés – Uluru, Kata Tjuta, the Kimberley, the Great Barrier Reef, rearing kangaroos, unnaturally alert koalas and painted aborigines. Turn the greens to brown, set the flesh on sand, turn the dancers into sportsmen clasped in the embrace of combat and what you have here is an image of Australia. What QANTAS is inviting us to discover, then, is not what we don't know about South America but what we already know about Australia.

This kind of ignorance about Latin America has long been and is still regarded not as a significant gap in one's knowledge but as a prerequisite for any real understanding of the continent. Ignorance furnishes a convenient and entirely reasonable pretext for dismissing the embodied evidence about Latin America, for disappearing its stubborn corporeality, and seeing it instead as the place where desires, fears and fantasies, prefabricated in and imported from home, might be realised or resolved. For Evelyn Waugh in the 1930s British Guyana was, as a "large map" of the country revealed, a patchwork of "blanks and guesses" (13). It was this nothingness and the lack of knowledge it embodied that attracted Waugh to Guyana in the first place and crucially shaped his responses to the country thereafter. In flight from a broken marriage and "the pervading savagery of civilized life" (Cunningham 53) Guyana is, in Waugh's vision, chiefly distinguishable by what it is not, by what its land, its settlements and its people lack – its qualities manifest in the roll call of its deficiencies:

> gradually a vague general idea began to take shape in my mind of a large *empty* territory stretching up three great rivers and their tributaries to shadowy *un*defined boundaries; most of it was *un*developed and *un*surveyed, large areas quite *un*explored; except for a trace of grassland

on the Brazilian frontier, and an inhabited fringe along the coast, it was all forest or swamp; there was *no* railway or road into the interior, the only means of communication being by boat up rivers broken every few miles by rapids and falls; the coast population contained every conceivable race, chiefly Portuguese, Negro and East Indian; the greater part of the colony had *no* permanent inhabitants ... except on the coast there had been practically *no* European settlement and little enough there. (Waugh 13. My italics)

For a man sickened by the polite cruelties of civilised society, "a shocked refugee from English social savagery and marital casualness", this catalogue of negations comprises Waugh's version of the vision splendid (Cunningham 82). Waugh's representations of Guyana were, as such, dictated by the need he had of it, his vision of the country fashioned by his rejection of England and the corrupted civilisation he associated it with. His vision of Guyana, a masterwork of blindness and prejudice, is thus a faithful, if inverse, portrait of England and all that he had rejected.

The explicit target of Cannadine's assertion that the empire was dedicated to the domestication of the exotic through parallel, analogy and equivalence is, of course, Edward Said. Said's reading of the British Empire conceived of it as a bureaucratic and discursive system designed to "other" and thereby legitimate the oppression of its subject peoples.[1] Cannadine contends that this approach is "too simplified" and Cannadine is not alone in his recognition that for all his moral forcefulness – if not because of it – Said's understanding of the relations between coloniser and colonised lacks subtlety, that it leans too heavily on Althusser and not nearly enough on Gramsci, and that as a result it is unable to acknowledge "the extent to which empire was about collaboration and consensus as well as about conflict and coercion" (*Ornamentalism* xvi).[2]

In the light of this it is something of a surprise to find Alan Knight, Professor of the History of Latin America at the University of Oxford, lamenting the lack of a "New World equivalent of Edward Said's 'Orientalism'". While "the stereotypes and prejudices catalogued by Said have their New World counterparts", there has, Knight ruefully points out, been no Latin Americanist critique of their origins and structure (2). The result of this lack is evident in the dispiriting caricatures that dominate British perceptions of Latin America, breed further ignorance and so entrench domestic indifference about the continent and its people. The British, as Knight observes, have a long and venerable "tradition of denigrating Latin America and its inhabitants" (3). In 1850, Palmerston grouped South America with China and Portugal as "half-civilised governments [... that] require a dressing down every eight or ten years to keep them in order [since] their minds are too shallow to receive any impression that will last longer than some such period. They care little for words and they must not only see the stick but actually feel it on their shoulders" (Miller 51). One hundred and fifty years later, though we are, as Knight reflects, "more polite, more politically correct [...] the incomprehension and stereotypes remain, even where least expected" (5). The pomp and panoply of empire may be gone but the attitudes that characterised and sustained it have turned out to be unexpectedly enduring. Knight longs for an academic avenger, a *Said ex-machina* as it were, to expose these stereotypes, the torturers and *tangueros*, soccer fiends and *sicarios*, drug barons, despots and displaced Nazis who inhabit British popular perceptions of the continent and its people for the risible caricatures they are and pack them off with their confreres in colonial condescension, the lustful Oriental, the physical African and the grateful slave. Yet as Cannadine's analysis implies, an Orientalist approach to western constructions of Latin America (a "tropicalism" perhaps?) would merely exchange one cast of caricatures for another – the feckless or malevolent giving place to the hoodwinked and oppressed.[3] Put simply, Knight's solution to colonial stereotyping looks suspiciously like postcolonial stereotyping. What to do?

I believe that we need to expend less energy on unmasking and condemning these stereotypes and more on achieving a better understanding of their origins and in particular their functions. And this is where Cannadine's analysis is of particular interest. It is his conviction that the process by which the British perceived and made sense of their far flung colonies, by apprehending the foreign in terms of the local and familiar, rescued their vision of the empire from trite reductivism, producing a sophisticated understanding of its structural complexities and a genuine responsiveness to the lives of the individuals who constituted it. Yet when this same sense-making system was applied to British visions of Latin America it rendered a disappointing array of othered familiars: where one promoted knowledge through identification the other fostered only ignorance. Why was it that an identical process resulted in such contrasting outcomes? The answer is hinted at in Elliott's observation that a society engaged in a genuine effort to comprehend another must undergo an often agonizing self-appraisal in which many "traditional preconceptions and inherited ideas" have to be jettisoned (15). As Peter Winch noted: "Seriously to study another way of life is necessarily to seek to extend our own – not simply to bring the other way within the already existing boundaries of our own because the point about the latter in their present form, is that they *ex hypothesi* exclude the other" (30). This is not a process that most societies will undertake lightly and, when it does take place it is driven, in the main, Elliott argues, not by altruism or a disinterested desire for greater knowledge of others but by a combination of compulsion and self-interest. In the case of the Spanish conquest of Latin America:

> ultimately it was the stimulus of practical considerations – the need to exploit the resources of America and to govern and convert its peoples – which compelled Europeans to widen their field of vision (sometimes in spite of themselves) and to organize and classify their findings within a coherent frame of thought.

> Officials and missionaries alike found that, to do their work effectively, they needed some understanding of the customs and traditions of the peoples entrusted to their charge [...] The *visitas* of royal officials to Indian localities therefore tended to turn into elaborate inquiries into native history, land tenure and inheritance laws; and the reports of the more intelligent and inquiring of these officials [...] were in effect exercises in applied anthropology, capable of yielding a vast amount of information about native customs and societies. (32–3)

The eagerness of the British to conquer and then exploit their imperial possessions, particularly in India, gave rise to practical considerations of government, commerce and comparative religion comparable to those that the Spaniards had confronted in the New World and that, albeit involuntarily, enforced a corresponding extension of the conquerors' cognitive boundaries. Yet in Latin America, while the British had extensive resources to exploit they had no people to govern and so no need to pretend to an interest in or concern for the locals and their culture, or any mission beyond the extraction of maximum profits. Freed from most of the "practical considerations" which might demand an uncomfortable cohabitation with the other, the British were under no compulsion to study the histories, societies and cultures of the Latin Americans, they had no need to expand their settled patterns of thought and perception to make room for the challenges posed by contact with them, and so no reason to subject themselves to a painful process of reappraisal. As such, while Latin America remained (and remains) of largely commercial interest to the British their prejudices about it could survive undisturbed.

If this helps explain the patterns of thinking which underlay British prejudices about Latin America and the reasons for their persistence, in what follows I will attempt a study of just one of the narratives which enshrine and articulate these prejudices. In doing so I will argue that what the dominant English-speaking communities know (or think they know) about Latin America is a function of the shifting needs and changing preoccupations of their own communities over this period – that Latin America as we know (or think we know) it is an invention, manufactured by and in the interests of the west. What I am attempting, as such, is a critique of western epistemologies of Latin America. I will proceed, therefore, in J. H. Elliott's terms, not by wrenching at the shutters for a glimpse of what is really out there but by turning my attention to the half-dark we have been stumbling around in, peering into and illuminating the gloom, sweeping away the cobwebs to get a clearer look at the mental furnishings which have cloaked our perceptions of Latin America for so long. Let me illustrate.

Alan Knight observes that the familiar stereotypes of Latin America are not only long-lived and difficult to shift, but that they also turn up in the most unexpected places and come from sources that really should know better. In evidence he cites Anthony Pagden's review of Volume VII of the *Cambridge History of Latin America* which, Knight claims:

embodied a farrago of familiar stereotypes. Pagden's Latin America is one of "chaos and political conflict"; of "near permanent civil war"; given to "bizarre games of politics"; lacking "established political parties or sophisticated political classes" [...] Latin American élites are, for Pagden, cultural quislings who speak "a hideous hybrid Spanglish", who drink Coca-Cola and eat cornflakes for breakfast. (7)[4]

What is most striking and ultimately most revealing about this review, is its source. Pagden, a fellow of King's College Cambridge, is a respected historian of early modern Spanish imperialism with a number of well-received books on the topic to his name.[5] He is, as such, if only by default, a Latin Americanist. Yet Malcolm Deas argues that Pagden's opinions demonstrate a profound ignorance about contemporary Latin America. His "ideas on the economic development of the region are so crude that one must seriously doubt that he has read the volume of the *Cambridge History of Latin America* that he is ostensibly reviewing" (4). Pagden proffers the kind of "worn-out received ideas" that would be rejected out of hand in relation to any other country but which are accepted as self-evident truths about Latin America: "'Certainly, the United States has never taken a benevolent or a sophisticated view of the political processes in Latin America (or, indeed, anywhere else in the world) [...]' What arrogant rubbish. Certainly? Never? Anywhere else in the world? Would you have printed that sentence in a review about 'anywhere else in the world?' I think not" (4). Deas's point here is not only that much of what Pagden had to say was "arrogant rubbish", but that nobody at the *London Review of Books* saw fit to challenge it, or seemed able, where Latin America is concerned, to distinguish ignorance from information, opinion from obloquy.

Alan Knight's exasperation stems not only from Pagden's unappetising display of prejudice but from his conviction that the review had failed in its primary duty, that it was "one of those reviews which tell you nothing about the book but a good deal about the reviewer" (6–7). (Are there any other kind?) The subtext here is almost audible. "If only he had stuck to the topic and kept his personal opinions in check we might have actually learnt something". Albeit inadvertently, Knight has put his finger here on the real significance of the review, that though it may say little of value about Latin America it implies a good deal about Anthony Pagden and perhaps even more about the forces which have shaped his, and our own views of the continent. In J. H. Elliott's phrase, again, the review briefly illuminates the half-light of his mental world and gives us a tantalising view of the furnishings. To appreciate what Pagden sees through the shutters we must first understand how this is linked to and informed by what he sees around him, how his responses to Latin America were filtered through and founded on the evidence of national decline and social fragmentation in the UK.

Seven months after Margaret Thatcher's strategic withdrawal from 10 Downing Street on 28 November 1990, (to an address somewhere to the right of General Pinochet), when Pagden's review appeared in the *London Review of Books*, the legacy of her eleven-and-a-half years in office was already clearly in evidence. By the late 1980s, as Arthur Marwick observed, "British society was more polarized than at any time since 1939" and "the country was clearly a disturbed place in which to live" (392, 366).[6] Thatcherism brought about revolutionary change in all areas of British life, so much so that according to John Gray of the London School of Economics, it ultimately swept away the very institutions, ideals and self-image which the Conservative Party had traditionally embodied and had pledged itself to defend:

> Thatcher was possessed by a vision of a country whose institutions had been ruthlessly reshaped but whose character remained miraculously unaltered. Markets were injected into hospitals and universities, council tenants were chivvied into buying their homes, public services were scorned as feckless repositories of unthinking compassion, and job insecurity was intensified for a host of occupations and professions. No corner of British life was left undisturbed.
>
> Despite all the social dislocations that these policies produced, the conservatives imagined Britain would still somehow be the place mocked in post-war Ealing films, a nation of stoical conformists bicycling impassively around changeless village greens.
>
> This picture may have had a faint semblance of reality in the Britain of the 1950s and 1960s that had been moulded into something approaching one nation by the reforming Labour government of 1945. By the time [John] Major left office [in May 1997] it was little more than a confection of the Tory media. In combination with vast changes in the world economy, Conservative policies had undone the social and family structures that underpinned pre-Thatcher Britain. (12)

Seated at High Table in King's College, witnessing the break up of "old national loyalties and communal networks", the demise of Margaret Thatcher and her succession by – of all people – John Major, the steady advance of the Coca-Cola drinkers and cornflakes jockeys, whatever his political affiliations, Pagden could be forgiven for believing that the country he thought he knew was collapsing all around him (Marwick 352). What is less forgivable, though perfectly understandable in the light of his ignorance, is his subsequent projection of his anxieties about developments in his own community onto his perceptions of Latin America. A fissile society increasingly divided along the fault lines of class, ethnicity and region; arrogance and corruption in government; growing extremes of poverty and wealth; an explosion in violent crime; increased drug and alcohol abuse; family breakdown; falling educational standards and a dramatic decline in the life expectancy of the poor. These are among the salient political and social failures of Britain in the late 1980s and early 90s, failures which Pagden projects onto Latin America in his review, where, to the evident irritation of Deas and Knight, they are magnified and distorted into the portrait of a permanent culture of deprivation, chaos and incompetence. Evidently, Pagden's Latin America is cast in the mould of his British preoccupations. The shock cities of the New World, their *barrios, favellas* and *poblaciones* are, to Pagden, scarcely distinguishable from the depressed towns and desolate public housing estates of the UK and the political and social failures they enshrine. What he sees through the shutters, then, is fundamentally shaped by what inhabits the half-light of his own mental world. In that regard he is a true son of Hernán Pérez de Oliva, giving "to those strange lands the form of his own", and thereby a loyal subject of the empire which, though politically defunct, remains a potent discursive force.

Pagden's review and my earlier observations on the Falklands War demonstrate therefore that as the preoccupations of our domestic world shift focus or change emphasis, as we worry about war, peace, prosperity, decline, the white man's burden or the end of empire, so our representations of Latin America shift also, regardless of conditions on the ground there at the time. Accordingly, Latin America as we know or think we know it through the literature, visual arts and media of the English-speaking west is fundamentally an invention of the west, a projection of what we know or think we know about ourselves, a register of our own passing concerns and collective preoccupations.

As interesting as I hope this is, it is not, sadly, an original insight. J. H. Elliott has noted how sixteenth-century representations of the New World as a rediscovered Eden had their origins in "Fifteenth-century Christendom's own sense of self-dissatisfaction [...] With the discovery of the Indies and their inhabitants [...] it was all too easy to transpose the ideal world from a world remote in time to a world remote in space. Arcadia and Eden could now be located on the far shores of the Atlantic" (25). Yet it wasn't only religious communities who sought an escape from the corruptions of the old world in an imagined vision of the new. The early humanists' vision of the new world grew out of and "enabled them to express their deep dissatisfaction with European society, and to criticise it by implication" (26). Peter Martyr's idealisation of the Indies in the *Decades* (1555) is premised on and shaped by the specific details of his disillusionment with the corruption, greed, deceit and divisions of Europe. Here, he declared, are people who live without weights and measures, without "pestiferous moneye, the seed of innumerable myscheves [...] without enforcement of lawes, without quarrelling Iudges and libelles, contente onely to satisfie nature, without further vexation for knowledge of thinges to come" (71).

As Peter Martyr's account implies, and as Sir Thomas More has demonstrated at some length in *Utopia* (1516), for sixteenth-century Europeans Latin America did not merely offer a refuge from the failings of the old world, it also served as an imaginary space in which the origins of those failings might be identified and a range of possible responses to them explored. As we enter the twenty-first century, while Latin America may no longer be the ideological battlefield of the great powers, it continues to serve as an intellectual playground for the west, the locus of its most optimistic imaginings and the embodiment of its deepest collective fears. As such, what we know about Latin America is still largely a function of what we know, what we think we know or what we wish we did or did not know about ourselves.

Works Cited

Ahmed, Leila. *Women and Gender in Islam: Historical Roots of a Modern Debate.* New Haven: Yale University Press, 1992.

Alomes, Stephen. "The British Press and Australia: Post-Imperial Fantasy and the Contemporary Media." *Meanjin* 46: 2 (1987): 173–83.

Aparicio, Frances R., and Susana Chávez-Silverman, eds. *Tropicalizations: Transcultural Representations of Latinidad.* Hanover, NH: University Press of New England, 1997.

Barnett, Anthony. *Iron Britannia.* London: Allison and Busby, 1982.

Bartlett, Frederick C. *Remembering: A Study in Experimental and Social Psychology.* Cambridge: Cambridge University Press, 1972.

Bhabha, Homi "Difference, Discrimination, and the Discourse of Colonialism." *The Politics of Theory.* Eds. F. Barker, P. Hulme, M. Iversen and D. Loxley. Colchester: University of Essex Press, 1983. 194–211.

Cannadine, David. *Class in Britain.* London: Penguin, 1998.

——. *Ornamentalism: How the British Saw their Empire.* London: Allen Lane, 2001.

Clarke, Peter. *Hope and Glory: Britain 1900–1990.* London: Penguin, 1996.

Cunningham, Valentine. *British Writers of the Thirties.* Oxford: Oxford University Press, 1989.

Curteis, Ian. *The Falklands Play.* London: Hutchinson, 1987.

Deas, Malcolm. "Unfair to Latin America." *London Review of Books* 14, 27 June 1991: 4.

Elliott, J. H. *The Old World and the New 1492–1650.* Cambridge: Cambridge University Press, 1970.

Gray, John. "Britain's Tories Flirting with Self-destruction." *The Guardian Weekly* 28 Sept. 1997: 12.

Knight, Alan. *Latin America: What Price the Past? An Inaugural Lecture Delivered Before the University of Oxford on 18 November 1993.* Oxford: Clarendon Press, 1994.

Loomba, Ania. *Colonialism/Postcolonialism.* London: Routledge,1998.

Maclachlan, Gale, and Ian Reid. *Framing and Interpretation.* Melbourne: Melbourne University Press, 1994.

Marwick, Arthur. *British Society Since 1945.* London: Penguin, 1990.

Martyr, Peter *Decades.* Trans. Richard Eden. *The First Three English Books on America.* Ed. Edward Arber. Birmingham: Turnbull and Spears, 1885.

Miller, Rory. *Britain and Latin America in the Nineteenth and Twentieth Centuries.* Harlow: Longmans, 1993.

More, Thomas. *Utopia.* Harmondsworth: Penguin, 1961.

Morgan, Kenneth S. *The Falklands Campaign: A Digest of Debates in the House of Commons 2 April to 15 June 1982.* London: HMSO, 1982.

Pagden, Anthony. "Basismo." Rev. of *The Cambridge History of Latin America*, vol.7, ed. by Leslie Bethel, *Magical Reels: A History of Cinema in Latin America*, by John King, and *Democracy and Development in Latin America: Economics, Politics and*

Religion in the Post-war Period, by David Lehman. *London Review of Books* 13 June 1991: 26–27

Porter, Dennis "*Orientalism* and its Problems", *The Politics of Theory*, Eds. F. Barker, P. Hulme, M. Iversen and D. Loxley. Colchester: University of Essex Press, 1983. 179–93.

Said, Edward. *Culture and Imperialism*. London: Chatto and Windus, 1993.

——. *Orientalism*. London: Penguin, 1978.

Waugh, Evelyn. *Ninety-Two Days*. London: Penguin, 1934.

Winch, Peter. "Understanding a Primitive Society." *Religion and Understanding*. Ed. D. Z. Phillips. Oxford: Oxford University Press, 1967. 9–42.

Notes

[1] For more on this see Said (1978) and (1993).

[2] Homi Bhabha criticised Said's promotion of a static model of colonial relations in which "colonial power and discourse is possessed entirely by the coloniser", and where there is no room for negotiation, compromise or change (200). See also Ahmed's claim that Said offers an overly homogenized representation of "the West", and Porter's assertion that Said's reduction of East-West relations to an entrenched system of binaries overlooks the subtle nuances in the shifting relations between them over a vast stretch of time. See Loomba for a crisp synopsis of these debates.

[3] Frances R. Aparicio and Susana Chávez-Silverman employ the term "tropicalism" to describe "the system of ideological fictions with which the dominant (Anglo and European) cultures trope Latin America and U.S. Latino/a identities and cultures" (1). The term is, as Aparicio and Chávez-Silverman concede, highly contested. For a more thorough definition of this understanding and use of the term, see Aparicio (8–10).

[4] Malcolm Deas was outraged by Pagden's stereotyping in which he detected not merely ignorance, "a parade of worn-out received ideas about Latin America" but contempt and a barely concealed racism: "Why not just call them poor benighted dagoes and have done?" (4).

[5] Pagden's books include *Spanish Imperialism and the Political Imagination* (1982) and *The Fall of Natural Man* (1990).

[6] According to Peter Clarke: "By any test, from statistical surveys of relative incomes to the striking reappearance of beggars on the streets, Britain [under Thatcher] became a more unequal society" (400).

The Tango Space of Argentina

Faye Bendrups

The collective mythology that conjures up tango and Argentine-ness can be directly traced to specific geographical contributors and the response to, and expression of, that space. That space is derived from physical locations and the crossings between them: in particular, the empty space of the interior and the crowded urban space of the city of Buenos Aires. Anthony Giddens suggests that space cannot "cause" or determine anything of itself: "To speak of 'space' in the context of geography is in fact to broach a series of concerns to do with the arrangement of persons and objects in the physical world" (cited in Werlen xv). The popular cultural phenomenon of tango can be seen as an expression of specific social situations of people in particular locations. That is, tango can be regarded as having logically evolved from transient populations' responses to an historic, spatially-derived sense of loss, failure and dislocation, which they encountered in the rural and urban landscapes of Argentina. Therefore, tango and Argentina can both be seen as existing at the level of the social imaginary as well as concretely. The arrangements of their interrelated cultural identities evolved from concerns of people and their habits, and they both may be effectively investigated according to Rob Shields's paradigm of "social spatialisation". Shields refers to the cultural logic of the spatial and other connected expressions in language, actions, and institutional arrangements as an encompassing frame of reference in the study of an object: "I use the term social spatialisation to designate the ongoing social construction of the spatial at the level of the social imaginary (collective mythologies, presuppositions) as well as interventions in the landscape (for example, the built environment)" (31). Following Shields's concept of social spatialisation, tango and Argentina can be investigated in relation to the geo-social sites of the interior and the littoral. In such a framework, manifestations of tango's concrete and abstract identity can be seen as powerfully emblematic of Argentina and Argentine identity.

The Empty Space

The tango-space association with the city of Buenos Aires is evident and clearly documented in tango literature and lyrics. The connection with the interior is less obvious, founded more on characteristics derived from the historical and social experiences of early Spanish colonial settlement. The environment encountered by Spanish colonial settlers in the sixteenth century was a vast and empty space. The conqueror had sought glory and wealth but the region which came to be called Argentina offered none, and the settlers' expectations of power and prosperity were unfulfilled. Filtered through the lens of the conquistador, this empty space became a social determinant at odds with its physical reality. It was a potentiality rather than an actuality; yielding disappointment. Similarly, in the seventeeth and eighteenth centuries, rupture and displacement continued to be the experience of a nation of oppressed and shifting peoples such as indigent and black slave populations. This sense of rupture and displacement is embodied in the tango dance. Ezequiel Martínez Estrada contends that tango is for people who seek escape in nirvana: "It is to evade the world" (*X-Ray* 257). He ascribes characteristics of the landscape, the plains, and cattle, to tango and likens the dance to the tedium of rural life:

> Melancholy originates from that repetition, from that contrast which results from seeing two bodies, built for free movement, subjected to the fatidic mechanical march of a beast of burden. It is the same sorrow we feel upon seeing young horses tied to a hoisting machine. (257)

Martínez Estrada describes the tango dance moves as "slow, with the feet dragging and with the pace of a grazing ox" and the bodies are "united, fixed, and adhere to each other like coupling insects". The tango music is described as "reminiscent of rumination" and the bandoneon "emits the sound of a moo" (259–260). The music is also fantasy, "like a narcotic", taking possession of the whole being. This engenders a kind of barren passivity: "To the beat of the tango it is possible to arrest thought and to float the soul in the body, as the fog wafts over the plain" (261). Martínez Estrada argues that the spell of the dance lies in its oblivion, its obliteration of will: "The tango is the dance of pessimism [...] a dance of the never-changing, enormous plains and of a subjugated and burdened race that crisscrosses them without end and without destiny, in the eternity of a forever repeating present" (257).

These descriptions of tango clearly evoke an association with the space encountered by the Spanish conquistador. Instead of El Dorado, they found a vast, featureless, dominating landscape peopled sparsely with "savage" Indians. The conquistador also discovered an interminable horizon of mirages: a false perception of a physical reality. The gaze might stretch to the horizon, but that was always unreachable and shifting. The land was unpredictable and untameable. Conditions such as fierce wildfires, thunderstorms, droughts and floods periodically drove settlers or workers to escape. Therefore, transience became a customary reponse to adversity, and the limitless landscape made this avoidance-escape option more attractive. The empty space of dust, vast horizons and endlessness contributed to a sense of impotence and displacement. V. S. Naipaul refers to the Argentine land-space as shaping a sense of alienation. The social contract in Argentina is not with each other, he argues, but with "the rich land, the precious commodity" (150). Land was seen as an investment, a hedge against inflation. Naipaul contends this resulted in an absence of history, shared ideals and community:

> In Argentina, unmade, flawed from its conception, without a history, still only with annals, there can be no feeling for a past, for a heritage, for shared ideals, for a community of all Argentines. Every Argentine wants to ratify his own contract with the God-given land, miraculously cleansed of Indians and still empty. (151)

Naipaul maintains that the land became no-one's home: "Home is elsewhere: Buenos Aires, England, Italy, Spain. You can live in Argentina, many Argentines say, only if you leave" (150). Martínez Estrada similarly argued that space triumphed over human dreams in this "featureless world, a world that imposed its hollow and fleshless reality [upon man]" (*X-Ray* 20–22) and that disapppointment, transience and the harshness of the environment were significant determinants in the shaping of identity:

> Thus the physical environment triumphed over ambition and forced it to be content with what nature offered: grain and cattle. More than that, the ambitious man was forced to accept a set of terrible conditions: a vagabond spirit, the zeal for accumulating things, the worship of quantity and size, the haste to leave, the disgrace of poverty, the breaking up of the home, the impossibility of a culture based on respect alone, and the emptiness of love. (20)

A sense of grief and loss, characteristics which imbue tango lyrics and music, may be causally related to insecurities founded on a spatial logic of such void. The emptiness of the Argentine landscape is described by Philip Guedalla: "There is nothing to record. It has no secrets since there are no folds in it where anything could be concealed" (235). Similarly, Christopher Isherwood wrote in his South American diary, *The Condor and the Cows*, that "It is a blank canvas upon which you have to do all the painting yourself, right up from the basic outlines. Nature provides no background, gives no helpful hints" (177). The vacant space of the interior was also seen as the space of backwardness. It was home to the "*gente perdida*" (forerunners of the gauchos) in the seventeenth century. It was a haven for outcasts and lower castes such as freed slaves, escaped conscripts and foreign deserters. It was the destination of seasonal farm workers from Europe who came to "*hacer la América*" – make their fortune – in the nineteenth century. These latter workers were named "*golondrinas*". Like transitory migrating birds, they flew in and flew out, as described in the 1934 tango song "Golondrinas":

> Golondrinas de un solo verano,
> con ansias constantes de cielo lejano
> Alma criolla, errante y viajera,
> querer detenerla es una quimera. (Merly 26)

The endless space of the interior was also a space of abandonment. It was left behind or departed from in substantial waves of internal migration from the interior to the littoral in the late nineteenth and early twentieth centuries. Representations of loss, dispossession and impermanence permeated nostalgic popular cultural expressions of gauchoesque poetry and literature, milonga and tango, even if these were mythologised re-constructions by literate city-dwellers. Country and city fused in compositions such as Bardi's "El buey solo" and "El rodeo" and Yupanqui's "Los ejes de mi carreta". The interior, and expressions of loss and uncertainty associated with it, were described sentimentally in tango songs like "Adiós pampa mía" (described on the sheet music edition as a "*tango campero*"). The singer speaks of the beloved ground of the pampa, the wind's song and the sobbing guitars:

> Con el canto de tus vientos
> y el sollozar de vihuelas
> que me alegraron a veces
> y otras me hicieron llorar.
>
> ¡Adiós, pampa mía!...
> Me voy camino de la esperanza.

In a romantic salutation, the singer attests to his love of the land and that away from the pampa, life is nothing. The memory of his past in the pampa is all:

> Adiós, caminos que he recorrido,
> ríos, montes y cañadas,
> tapera donde he nacido.
> Si no volvemos a vernos,
> tierra querida,
> quiero que sepas
> que al irme dejo la vida.
> ¡Adiós!... (Gobello 250)

Buenos Aires: The Promissory Metropolis

In the nineteenth and twentieth centuries the city of Buenos Aires became the dominant site of development and change in Argentina. A sense of imbalance arose between the rapid expansion of an out-of-balance metropolis and the abandonment of the empty space of the interior, as the population of Buenos Aires grew to roughly a third of the whole of Argentina. The unwieldy and uncontrolled metropolis, which was referred to as "Babylon" by Eduardo Mallea, "La cabeza de Goliat" by Martínez Estrada, and "Babel" by Albert Londres, became the central site for people seeking their fortunes, from both within and outside Argentina. However, class divides and a powerful oligarchy sustained an inequitable society, and few succeeded.

In the late 1800s and the early 1900s, migrants from Europe were attracted to Argentina by the lure of better wages, social advancement and business opportunities. Congress authorised the contracting in of migrant labour, setting up recruitment agents in Europe and providing establishment incentives for new workers. Population growth was significant. In 1857 the population of Argentina was 1.1 million, but by 1890 it had grown to 3.3 million, and the city grew at an unprecedented pace until the 1920s. The influx was not without conflict. Ruling classes were fearful of being displaced from power, and some native rural populations resorted to violent encounters (Rock, *Argentine* 142–43). David Rock describes the immigrant population as mobile, slow to organise, and with little political influence (*Argentine* 142–43. See also Weber and Rausch 73–83; Madsen and Snow 37). The immigrants were outsiders. They brought their old customs and habits to meld with the new. They were poor and powerless, but dreaming of wealth and opportunity. In the land of promise, they sought personal gain. Central to the identity of Buenos Aires is the effect of change, in areas such as trade and commerce, cultural and political life, and population shifts. Beatriz Sarlo states that the socio-economic processes which began in the last half of the nineteenth century changed not only the physical features of the city of Buenos Aires but the experiences of the inhabitants: "Así, Buenos Aires interesa como espacio físico y como mito cultural: ciudad y modernidad se presuponen porque la ciudad es el escenario de los cambios, los exhibe de manera ostensible y a veces brutal, los difunde y generaliza" (183).

Sarlo poses questions of a Buenos Aires identity and *porteño* values pertaining to broader social questions, particularly of access to and participation in civil society. She singles out conflict and constant change as determinants in the discourse of Buenos Aires experience. The effects of rapid change with limited urban planning controls resulted in a city of mixed styles and functions. The development of Buenos Aires is generally agreed to be random, without plan, and without a well-defined character and style. Richard J. Walter (252) comments on attempts at planning and regulation which were met with exceptions and evasions or lack of enforcement. He describes the development of Buenos Aires thus:

> Construction had been haphazard, without plan or aesthetic sense. Architectural styles were hopelessly jumbled and capriciously placed skyscrapers overshadowed other buildings of various shapes and sizes. There was too much improvisation, too much impermanence. The whole city, moreover, was too isolated and removed from the rest of Argentina. (252)

Martínez Estrada described Buenos Aires as a city "without secrets, without viscera or glands, without deep convolutions or caries. Everything is in the open; once the city is known on the outside, it ceases to interest. It lacks a yesterday and does not possess a true shape" (*X-Ray* 235). He suggested that Buenos Aires "absorbed" the whole republic of Argentina, being the rail, road and sea link with trade routed to Europe (*X-Ray* 226). The allure of

Buenos Aires was its monopoly over trade, political power, industrialisation and "civilisation". Commerce (import/export markets), the past (Europe and the Mother Country), development (local and foreign investment) and hope (expectation of "making it") were central to her existence.

The transmigration to the city was an inevitable next step for individuals seeking a better life, whether they came from the interior or from foreign lands. With "progress" comes opportunity, and Buenos Aires was seen as a promissory metropolis. The city became a fast urban centre mixing European customs, architecture and lifestyle, arterially linked to the pampa with dirt roads lined with adobe dwellings and disadvantage. Buenos Aires promised new challenges and adventures. In contrast, the interior was plainly and monotonously a location of hard work, ignorance and disillusionment. Buenos Aires therefore became more than just a physical place; it was also a site of dreams and aspirations, where fortunes could be made and freedom could be attained. In reality, few prospered, as the city offered the migrant little except crowded housing tenements, dirt floors and struggle. As a "monument to an aspiration" in Martínez Estrada's words (*X-Ray* 235), it succeeded as an edifice-sign emulating the beauty and progress of Paris, Berlin or New York. It failed also: in haphazard planning controls, buildings poorly constructed, mis-matches of styles, and inadequate plumbing and drainage.

Buenos Aires continues to be eulogised in the tango "Mi Buenos Aires querido", an anthem to the city as loved and familiar as the popular song "New York, New York" is in North America. "Mi Buenos Aires querido" tells of a city whose song "wipes out tears of pain":

> En la cortada más maleva una canción
> dice su ruego de coraje y de pasión
> una promesa
> y un suspirar
> borró una lágrima de pena aquel cantar.
> Mi Buenos Aires querido
> cuando yo te vuelva a ver
> no habrá más penas ni olvido. (Tedesco 40–41)

The kind of connection to place expressed by this popular tango is repeated in countless others. Tango mostly celebrates (sometimes berates) Buenos Aires, the roulette wheel upon which bets had been placed. If Buenos Aires failed to meet expectations of ambitious migrants, where else would? Instead of leaving in defeat, many stayed, proudly persistent and defiant. Buenos Aires, like New York, became an epithet that symbolised the aspirations of those in transit and seeking success. It would be acclaimed, loved, admired, applauded. Its attraction was the blend of opposing realities: the technical, physical, mechanical, ordered, repetitious, limited, rational world of everyday works and habits; and the world of escape: gossip, superstition, hopes, imaginings, chance (such as gambling, card games, lottery tickets), potential, or spiritual connection (Sebreli 175–76). In this latter world fit the tango: site of escape and dreams. The tango song "Buenos Aires" reveres the city as assuager of ills:

> Buenos Aires, la Reina del Plata
> Buenos Aires, mi tierra querida
> escuchá mi canción,
> que con ella va mi vida.
> En mis horas de fiebre y orgía,
> harto ya de placer y locura,
> yo pienso en ti, patria mía,
> para calmar mi amargura. (Couselo 14)

Whether, in fact, Buenos Aires could or could not calm the singer's bitterness is debatable. Certainly, the expectation that the city could function as a site of comfort was clearly expressed in countless tango songs. Tango lyrics document life in the barrios, particular locations, and offer an overview of the city. In this way, tango becomes a sociological chronicle of *porteño* life, describing not only the physical environment, but also the experiences and habits of people within particular places and social circumstances. The affection for one's birthplace is revealed in the tango "Puente Alsina", nostalgically reflecting on a romanticised past. The singer recounts how the suburb is being altered by the modernising march of progress, and contrasts this actuality with the consoling memories of "yesterday":

> ¿Dónde está mi barrio, mi cuna querida?
> ¿Dónde la guarida, refugio de ayer?
> Borró el asfaltado, de una manotada,
> la vieja barriada que me vio nacer
>
>   *   *   *   *   *
>
> Puente Alsina, que ayer fuera mi regazo,
> de un zarpazo la avenida te alcanzó
>
>   *   *   *   *   *
>
> Viejo puente, solitario y confidente,
> sos la marca que, en la frente,
> el progreso le ha dejado
> al suburbio rebelando
> que a su paso sucumbió. (Gravina 170)

The tango "Milonga de mi barrio" also describes a place where life and love is nostalgically remembered. The neighbourhood is where the singer first fell in love and where his "saintly mother" first kissed him. He comes here to lament and to remember the past:

> ¡Vengo mi barrio a cantarte
> pa recordar el ayer!
> ¡Vengo a sentirme más tuyo
> Y más purrete a la vez! (Satur and Ponzio)

The lyrics of "Corrientes y Esmeralda" (1933), by Celedonio E. Flores and music by Francisco Pracánico, deliberately set out to immortalise the street intersection in tango song form, describing the nightlife, buskers, cinemas (Gravina 103). Other tangos like "El bulín de la calle Ayacucho" (1925), "Bajo Belgrano" (1926), "El cornetín del tranvía" (1937), "Caserón de tejas" (1941), "Las cuarenta" (1937), "Barrio de tango" (1942), "Cafetín de Buenos Aires" (1948), "San José de Flores" (1936), "Balada para un loco" (1969) and "Buenos Aires conoce" (1976) perpetuate Buenos Aires, her place names, street life and everyday customs in the tango cultural directory.

Tango Space: Physical and Metaphysical

The social and spatial Argentine experience was intertwined from the infinity of the interior to the closeness of the city and provided a contentious site for expressions of dreams. The elaboration of this experience in language, culture and custom was bound to the struggle over geography, a complex struggle that is of interest because, as Edward Said suggests: "it is not only about soldiers and cannons, but also about ideas, about forms, about images and imaginings" (6). In Argentina, the nostalgic sense of loss, transience and displacement which was produced by a correlation of responses to place and cultural expressions of these experiences, is narrated in tango song lyrics, poetry and literature. Tango also functions as a cultural construction reconciling the participant to the actuality of their broader social conditions. Tango helps to make these conditions – which may be overpowering and uncontrollable – accessible and bearable. The tango "Tango mío" expresses tango's brotherly function:

> Con una guitarra o un bandoneón
> canta tango hermano,
> canta tu canción.
> Y con las tristezas que te da la vida
> curarás la herida de tu corazón
> canta tu canción... (Ferrer and De Priore 201)

The sense of sadness and succour evoked in this song is typically associated with tango expressions. Scalabrini Ortiz refers to the music of tango as "lastimada y sencilla" and that the music "dice las amarguras de todos los porteños" (18). Enrique Santos Discépolo's definition of tango – "un pensamiento triste que se baila" – is described as the one most exact and essential by Ernesto Sábato (11). This sense of sadness is perhaps among the most recurrent characteristics of Argentine experience and identity. After six military coups throughout the twentieth century, even a return to democracy in 1983 could not assuage the habituation to inadequate civil governance and a continuing culture of corruption. Argentina was left economically and morally bankrupt and by 2002, the economy had collapsed after a world record default on the external debt. A newly-impoverished middle class took their pot-banging protests, known as *"cacerolazos"*, and public shaming – *"escraches"* – to the streets, institutions and private homes of the ruling class, demanding "que se vayan todos". The cultural phenomenon of tango – the artistic expression associated globally with Argentina, the fourth-largest export earner for the Argentine economy, and the metaphysical site of comfort and belonging to which Argentines could turn – could not compensate for the decline. Do the rich tango trappings of gaudy costumes, seductive gestures, tourist tours, glamourised promotions and the comforting trap of nostalgia, mask a poverty of identity? The French sociologist Alain Touraine described it thus: "Los argentinos existen; la Argentina, no" (5), or as a taxi driver remarked to this author in 2001: "Nosotros, los argentinos, somos una fantasía. Buenos Aires no existe". The tango space of Argentina, embodied with elements of the vast, empty plains of the interior and the unpredictability of the promissory metropolis, has become a limbo. We are yet to see whether tango, and by extrapolation Argentina, will have the creative fortitude to revivify a cultural identity that has become trapped in repetition, or whether it will implode tanguistically in sorrowful oblivion?

Works cited

Couselo, Jorge Miguel. *Manuel Romero cancionero*. Buenos Aires: Torres Agüero, 1982.

Ferrer, Horacio, and Oscar Del Priore. *Inventario del tango*. 2 vols. Buenos Aires: Fondo Nacional de las Artes, 1999.

Gobello, José. *Letras de tangos*. Buenos Aires: Nuevo Siglo, 1977.

Gravina, Alfredo, ed. *El tango ayer y hoy*. La Habana: Casa de las Américas, 1984.

Guedalla, Philip. *Argentine Tango*. London: Hodder and Stoughton, 1932.

Isherwood, Christopher. *The Condor and the Cows*. London: Methuen, 1949.

Londres, Albert. *The Road to Buenos Ayres*. Trans. Eric Sutton. London: Constable, 1928.

Madsen, Douglas, and Peter G. Snow. *The Charismatic Bond*. Cambridge, MASS: Harvard University Press, 1996.

Mallea, Eduardo. *Historia de una pasión argentina*. Buenos Aires: Sudamericana, 1975.

Martínez Estrada, Ezequiel. *La cabeza de Goliat; microscopía de Buenos Aires*. Madrid: Ediciones de la Revista de Occidente, 1970.

——. *X-Ray of the Pampa*. Trans. Alain Swietlicki. Austin: University of Texas Press, 1971.

Merly, Oriana, ed. *200 Tangos*. Caracas: ABCD, 1985.

Naipaul, V. S. *The Return of Eva Perón*. New York: Knopf, 1980.

Rock, David. *Argentina 1516–1987: From Spanish Colonization to Alfonsín*. Berkeley: University of California Press, 1987.

——. *Authoritarian Argentina*. Berkeley: University of California Press, 1995.

Sábato, Ernesto. *Tango: discusión y clave*. Buenos Aires: Losada, 1963.

Said, Edward. *Culture and Imperialism*. London: Chatto and Windus, 1993.

Sarlo, Beatriz. "Modernidad y mezcla cultural." *Buenos Aires 1880–1930. La capital de un imperio imaginario.* Ed. Horacio Vázquez-Rial. Madrid: Alianza, 1996. 183–95.

Scalabrini Ortiz, Raúl. *El hombre que está solo y espera.* Buenos Aires: Librerías Anaconda, 1931.

Sebreli, Juan José. *Buenos Aires, vida cotidiana y alienación.* Buenos Aires: Siglo Veinte, 1964.

Shields, Rob. *Places on the Margin.* London: Routledge, 1991.

Tedesco, Luis Osvaldo, ed. *Alfredo Le Pera cancionero.* Buenos Aires: Torres Agüero, 1977.

Touraine, Alain. "La Argentina nunca se constituyó como sociedad." *La Nación* 27 de octubre de 2002: 5.

Walter, Richard J. *Politics and Urban Growth in Buenos Aires 1910–1942.* Cambridge: Cambridge University Press, 1993.

Weber, David J. and Jane M. Rausch, eds. *Where Cultures Meet: Frontiers in Latin American History.* Wilmington: Scholarly Resources, 1994.

Werlen, Benno. *Society, Action and Space: An Alternative Human Geography.* London: Routledge, 1993.

Presencia de los tangos en la poesía de Julio Cortázar

Guillermo Anad

Es archiconocida la pasión que Julio Cortázar (1914–1984) tuvo por el jazz. Uno de sus relatos más famosos, "El perseguidor", alude a Charlie Parker y *Rayuela* está repleta de referencias al jazz y al blues. Lo que no es tan conocido es que Cortázar, a lo largo de su producción literaria, nunca "perdió de oído" a la canción de Buenos Aires, y su presencia en distintos textos es más frecuente de lo que habitualmente se supone. Por otra parte, desde el poema "Tango" (1911) de Ricardo Güiraldes, es muy difícil encontrar a un escritor o una escritora bonaerense que no haya dicho lo suyo con, desde o alrededor del tango.

Este artículo tratará sobre poemas que Cortázar escribió basándose en los viejos tangos: "Rechiflao en mi tristeza", "Malevaje 76", "Veredas de Buenos Aires", "Quizás la más querida", "Milonga" y "Las tejedoras" de la sección "Con tangos" de *Salvo el crepúsculo* (1984) y "1950 año del Libertador, etc." de *La vuelta al día en ochenta mundos* (1967). Se observará aquí la importancia que le concedió Cortázar a la canción porteña, tanto en relación a su propio lenguaje como escritor, como a la inestimable posibilidad de entablar (a través del tango) un diálogo profundo y cercano con la sociedad argentina.

En efecto, en "1950 año del Libertador, etc." una línea del tango "Muñeca brava" (1929) le brindará a Cortázar la posibilidad de una demoledora crítica social. La alusión a Perón en el título, a través de la figura de San Martín, es tan clara como certera: el primer centenario de la muerte del General San Martín ocurre a fines del primer término del gobierno de Perón, quien desde 1948 era Gran Maestro de la Orden del Libertador San Martín. En 1950, el Congreso nacional impone la obligatoriedad del uso de la leyenda "Año del Libertador General José de San Martín" (Ciria 284). Por otra parte, el peronismo siempre ha querido ver una continuidad en la línea San Martín-Rosas-Perón. Son los tiempos "en que Perón desalojaba a Zeus para siempre de mi casa" (Cortázar, *Salvo* 341). "Y si el llanto te viene a buscar / escurrí tu dolor y reí [...] Meta champán / que la vida se te escapa [...]" decía el mencionado tango, con letra de Enrique Cadícamo (Tedesco, *Cadícamo* 23). A Cortázar – quien acababa de regresar de su primer viaje a Europa y estaba por alejarse nuevamente (y esta vez para siempre) de la Argentina, a punto de embarcarse para París en busca de "un estilo de vida que las calles del nuevo Buenos Aires peronista me negaban" (Cortázar, *Salvo* 329) – este tango le servirá para descargar su profundo rechazo a la sociedad argentina de la segunda posguerra y a la tan mentada "viveza criolla":

> Y si el llanto te viene a buscar
> agarralo de frente, bebé entero
> el copetín de lágrimas legítimas.
> Llorá, argentino, llorá por fin un llanto
> de verdad, cara al tiempo
> que escamoteabas ágilmente,
> llorá las desgracias que creías ajenas,
> la soledad sin remisión al pie de un río,
> la culpa de la paz sin mérito,
> la siesta de barrigas rellenas de pan dulce.
> (Cortázar, *Vuelta* 196)

Este poema integra la sección que lleva un título por demás elocuente, "Razones de la cólera". Las motivaciones y el estado de ánimo de Cortázar en la "Buenos Aires, capital del miedo" (Cortázar, *Salvo* 333), frente al país peronizado, están reflejadas en su comentario evocativo de la poesía y la vida intelectual en Buenos Aires por esos días: "Nuestra autocompasión presente en la poesía bonaerense de ese tiempo plagado de elegías, que en el fondo eran tangos con diploma de alta cultura, el mismo amargo regusto de nuestras frustraciones locales que se travestían con la involuntaria ayuda de los dior o los cardin importados por las modas poéticas del momento" (Cortázar, *Salvo* 337).

Pero no todo es disgusto: "Para mí, detrás de tanta cólera, el amor está allí desnudo y hondo como el río que me llevó tan lejos" se lee en *La vuelta al día en ochenta mundos* (195). Justamente en este libro – en un ensayo sobre Carlos Gardel – Cortázar comentará que el tango "Mano a mano" (1923), con letra de Celedonio Flores, es el que prefiere:

> a cualquier otro tango y a todas las grabaciones de Gardel [...] Tal vez prefiero este tango porque da la justa medida de lo que representa Carlos Gardel. Si sus canciones tocaron todos los registros de la sentimentalidad popular, desde el encono irremisible hasta la alegría del canto por el canto, desde la celebración de glorias turfísticas hasta la glosa del suceso policial, el justo medio en que se inscribe para siempre su arte es el de este tango casi contemplativo, de una serenidad que se diría hemos perdido sin rescate. (91)

Cortázar resalta el contraste que hay entre Gardel y Alberto Castillo, otro famoso cantante de tangos y gran exponente de lo que Juan José Sebreli, en *Los deseos imaginarios del peronismo* (1992), denominará "el dopolavorismo fascista:" "El desenfrenado Alberto Castillo gritando *Por cuatro días locos* no era sino la réplica chabacana del tenor Tito Schipa en *Vivere*, la canción de la alegría fascista" (100). Justamente, Cortázar deplora "la mera delectación en el mal gusto y la canallería resentida que explican el triunfo de un Alberto Castillo" (*Vuelta* 89).

Con respecto a "Mano a mano", tal será el apego de Cortázar por este tango que, muchos años después en 1976, de viaje por África oriental – más concretamente en Nairobi – lo utilizará para el intertexto en otro poema de identidad tanguina. Decía el tango de Flores: "Rechiflao en mi tristeza, hoy te evoco y veo que has sido / en mi pobre vida paria, sólo una buena mujer" (Castanedo García 238). Pues bien, sin llegar a la explícita confesión de Jack Kerouac, quien afirma en *Mexico City Blues* (1959) "I want to be considered a jazz poet blowing a long blues in an afternoon jam session on Sunday", Cortázar admite la inevitable asistencia de los tangos en determinados momentos. Este es el comentario – no exento de cierta ironía, por cierto – que precede al poema: "No sé en qué medida las letras del jazz influyen en los poetas norteamericanos, pero sí que a nosotros los tangos nos vuelven en una recurrencia sardónica cada vez que escribimos tristeza, que estamos llovizna, que se nos atasca la bombilla en la mitad del mate" (*Salvo* 69). "Mano a mano" será entonces el tango con el que Cortázar escribirá el suyo, "Rechiflao en mi tristeza":

> Te evoco y veo que has sido
> en mi pobre vida paria
> una buena biblioteca.
>
> Te quedaste allá,
> en Villa del Parque,
> con Thomas Mann y Roberto Arlt y Dickson Carr,
> con casi todas las novelas de Colette,
> Rosamond Lehmann, Charles Morgan, Nigel Balchin,
> Elías Castelnuovo y la edición
> tan perfumada del pequeño
> amarillo Larousse Ilustrado,
> donde por suerte todavía
> no había entrado mi nombre. (*Salvo* 69)

La expresión *mano a mano* implica una idea de balance y de equidad. En este sentido, es notable la paradigmática sustitución que realiza Cortázar: mientras que el tango de Flores se refería a la relación entre un hombre y una mujer, y a "la vida de una mujer que es una mujer de la vida" (*Vuelta* 91), en "Rechiflao en mi tristeza" el tema es la relación del escritor con la literatura y los "personajes" son los libros de un hombre que es un hombre de libros.

Otro de los clásicos de la canción rioplatense que citará Cortázar es el tango "Malevaje" (1928), con letra de Enrique S. Discépolo. El tanguero se lamentaba de la mujer que lo dejó y, entre otras cosas, decía "No me has dejao ni el pucho en la oreja / de aquel pasao malevo y feroz. Ya no me falta pa' completar / más que ir a misa e hincarme a rezar" (Tedesco, *Discépolo* 16). En "Malevaje 76", tango y blues se dan la mano:

> Como un cáncer que avanza
> abriéndose camino entre las flores

de la sangre, seccionando los nervios del deseo,
la azul relojería de las venas,

granizo de sutil malentendido,
avalancha de llantos a destiempo.

Para qué desandar la inútil ruta
que nos llevó a esta ciega
contemplación de un escenario hueco:

No me has dejao
ni el pucho en la oreja,
ya solamente sirvo
para escuchar a Carole Baker
entre dos tragos de ginebra,

y ver caer el tiempo
como un lluvia de polillas
sobre estos pantalones desplanchados. (*Salvo* 68)

También este tango lo escribió Cortázar en Kenya, como si por una mágica coincidencia, y desde un discurso "metatanguino" se pudiera invocar – aunque no quede más que en una especulación teórica – la afroargentinidad inmanente que tenía el tango en el siglo XIX. También notable en estos verdaderos *collages*, es el hecho de que Cortázar no diferencia tipográficamente los pasajes anexados. Una vez más, no hay comillas, no hay negrilla, de manera que la propuesta es evidentemente la de integrar el lenguaje del tango al discurso poético. Por otra parte, como bien lo señaló en 1949 en su crítica al *Adán Buenosayres* (1948) de Leopoldo Marechal, Cortázar siempre buscó esa síntesis que amalgamara los dos registros del idioma: el literario y el coloquial contenido en los tangos:

> Muy pocas veces entre nosotros se había sido tan valientemente leal a lo circundante, a las cosas que están ahí mientras escribo estas palabras, a los hechos que mi propia vida me da y me corrobora diariamente, a las voces y las ideas y los sentires que chocan conmigo y son yo en la calle, en los círculos, en el tranvía y en la cama. (*Obra* 171–72)

En "Veredas de Buenos Aires" resuenan los versos del tango "Tinta roja" (1941). Decía su autor Cátulo Castillo, "¿Dónde estará mi arrabal? / ¿Quién se robó mi niñez?" – y luego – "Veredas que yo pisé, / malevos que ya no son, / bajo tu cielo de raso / trasnocha un pedazo / de mi corazón" (Tedesco, *Castillo* 91). En sintonía nostálgica, rememorará Cortázar:

> De pibes la llamamos la vedera
> y a ella le gustó que la quisiéramos.
> En su lomo sufrido dibujamos
> tantas rayuelas.
>
> Después, ya más compadres, taconeando,
> dimos vueltas manzana con la barra,

silbando fuerte para que la rubia
del almacén saliera a la ventana.
A mí me tocó un día irme muy lejos
pero no me olvidé de las vederas.
Aquí o allá las siento en los tamangos
como la fiel caricia de mi tierra. (*Salvo* 72)

Una vez más, el tono es de un claro registro tanguino. Es notable el uso deliberado de argentinismos ("vedera" por vereda, entre otros), además de los títulos de dos famosos tangos, "Taconeando" (1930) y "Silbando" (1925), ambos grabados por el Gardel que prefería Cortázar, el Gardel con guitarras (*Vuelta* 89).

En relación al origen afroargentino del tango, tampoco faltó la milonga campera en la poesía de Cortázar. La milonga proviene de la payada, la cual es "a sort of poetic duel in which two guitarrist-singers spontaneously compose verses on a given theme or in response to each other's challenges. A vocal variation on the *tapadas*, the drum duels, the *payada* was the lineal descendant of the African tradition of musical contests of skill" (Andrews 170). Guitarra en mano, el payador se acompañaba para improvisar su canto. Uno de los más importantes payadores fue el afroargentino Gabino Ezeiza, quien además fue un notable poeta. En el poema "Un Oriental: ausente de su patria", Ezeiza expresaba un fuerte sentimiento de soledad y destierro: "Lejos, muy lejos me encuentro / de aquella patria querida, / cuyo recuerdo no olvida / mi doliente corazón. / Allí están mis ojos fijos / mi esperanza allí se encierra..." (citado en Lewis 123). En un tono similar, Cortázar escribe su poema "Milonga":

Extraño la Cruz del Sur
cuando la sed me hace alzar la cabeza
para beber tu vino negro medianoche.
Y extraño las esquinas con almacenes dormilones
donde el perfume de la yerba tiembla en la piel
del aire. (*Salvo* 75)

A través de los "almacenes dormilones", lugares de renunión típicamente orilleros, queda explicitada la nostalgia porteña por las noches pampeanas, tema no poco frecuente en los primeros tangos camperos.

En "Quizá la más querida", hay una alusión al tango "Cafetín de Buenos Aires" (1948), con letra de Enrique S. Discépolo. Este tango evoca un lugar lleno de amargura, desengaño y locura, con un alto contenido arltiano: "En tu mezcla milagrosa / de sabihondos y suicidas, / yo aprendí filosofía... dados... timba... / y la poseía cruel / de no pensar más en mí. / Me diste en oro un puñado de amigos, / [...] Sobre tus mesas que nunca preguntan / lloré una tarde el primer desengaño, / nací a las penas, bebí mis años [...]" (Tedesco, *Discépolo* 76–77). Cortázar comienza reescribiendo este ambiente, pero inmediatamente "el cafetín" mismo es ya signo de ausencia y abandono:

Me diste la intemperie,
la leve sombra de tu mano
pasando por mi cara.
Me diste el frío, la distancia,
el amargo café de medianoche
entre mesas vacías.

* * * * *

Fui una letra de tango
para tu indiferente melodía. (*Salvo* 73)

En los dos últimos versos del poema, el tango es el yo lírico que se ha quedado sin partitura. La sensación es de inconmensurable dolor.

El poema "Las tejedoras", se inscribe en el contexto de la endémica militarización y peronización de la sociedad argentina, el mismo marco referencial al que se alude en el primero de los poemas estudiados en este artículo: "1950 año del Libertador, etc". Se recordará que Gardel celebró el primer cuartelazo argentino que llevó a la presidencia al general Uriburu y del cual participaron los futuros presidentes, el general Agustín P. Justo y el entonces capitán Juan Perón. En efecto, el 6 de septiembre de 1930, la Argentina iniciaba así un camino sin retorno de permanente rechazo de la democracia. Pues bien, el tango que Gardel grabó se llamó "¡Viva la Patria!" (1930) y llevaba letra de Francisco García Jiménez. En la portada de la partitura de este tango se lee: "A la mujer, al ejército, al periodismo ilustre, a los prohombres, a la juventud universitaria, al pueblo todo [...] a todos los que aportaron un arma, un grito, o un gesto siquiera, a la conquista de la idea suprema, el 6 de septiembre de 1930". La trágica muerte de Gardel en 1935 en un accidente de avión le caerá como anillo al dedo al gobierno del general Justo para la construcción del mito. A Jorge Luis Borges, por su parte, la muerte de Gardel le conmoverá mucho menos que la de Almotásim El Magrebí, poeta apócrifo del siglo XII inventado por el mismo Borges, según Blas Matamoro (92). De todas maneras, el mito "gardeliano" que difunde la radio es ya imparable y "ser Gardel" será el mejor elogio para un argentino; el próximo mito colectivo y omnipresente será el de Evita Perón, a partir de la década del 50. Así, años más tarde, *el* Buenos Aires tan *querido* del tango de Gardel y Le Pera (nótese la masculinización de la ciudad) y la Argentina misma, le parecerán a V. S. Naipaul "an artificial, fragmented colonial society, made deficient and bogus by its myths" (115). Cortázar describía así a la sociedad de "la moral radiotelefónica" (*Salvo* 330):

Las conozco, las horribles, las tejedoras envueltas en pelusas,
en colores que crecen de las manos del hilo

* * * * *

en el espacio sucio de bocinas y lamentos de radio
en cada hueco donde el tiempo sea un pulóver.

* * * * *

Tejen olvido, estupidez y lágrimas

    *   *   *   *   *

¡Ahí vienen, vienen! Monstruos de nombre blando, tejedoras,
hacendosas mujeres de los hogares nacionales, oficinistas, rubias,
mantenidas, pálidas novicias. Los marineros tejen,
las enfermas envueltas en biombos tejen para el insomnio,
del rascacielo bajan flecos enormes de tejidos, la ciudad
está envuelta en lanas como vómitos verdes y violeta.
Ya están aquí, ya se levantan sin hablar,
solamente las manos donde agujas brillantes van y vienen,
y tienen manos en la cara, en cada seno tienen manos, son
ciempiés son cienmanos tejiendo en un silencio insoportable
de tangos y discursos. (*Último* 2: 208–11)

Se recordará que los discursos radiales de Perón empezaron en 1944 y a partir
de su primera presidencia en 1946, las radios estuvieron controladas por el
peronismo: "Argentine listeners soon consumed a steady diet of propaganda
extolling the president, his wife and their philosophy of government" (Page
210). Por su parte, un personaje de la novela *Los premios* (1960), rememorará
así a su ciudad: "las novelas en cadena oyendo roncar los ómnibus, la no
vida de un Buenos Aires sin futuro para ella, el tiempo plácido y húmedo, el
noticioso de Radio El Mundo" (87). Por último, mientras que entre 1947 y
1950 en la Argentina de los Perón se tejía una extensa red de migración nazi
(Martínez 193), la radio se convirtió en el principal medio de difusión de
mitos colectivos (Sebreli 81), así como también un gran factor de permanente
alienación.

Tanto la poesía de Cortázar como el tango que no es baile ni canción,
comparten el debatible privilegio de no haber logrado fama mundial, de estar
fuera del canon, de ser lo otro. Por cierto que los poemas aquí presentados
siempre han llegado bastante tarde a los libros de Cortázar y todavía más
tarde al mundo del tango (desentrañar las causas excedería largamente el
marco de esta nota). Por otra parte, los estudios académicos cortazarianos
se han centrado de manera casi excluyente en su narrativa, y, claro está, se
trata de su obra más voluminosa. Con todo, estos poemas *son* los tangos y
"contratangos" de un escritor que, al tiempo que realizaba un trascendente
aporte a la narrativa hispanoamericana, mantuvo también un estrecho
contacto con lo más argentino que el idioma le pudo haber brindado: los
viejos tangos.

Obras citadas

Andrews, George Reid. *The Afro-Argentines of Buenos Aires, 1800–1900*. Madison:
    University of Wisconsin Press, 1980.
Castanedo García, Federico, ed. *El tango: compilación de tangos antiguos y modernos*.
    México: Editora Latino Americana, 1966.

Ciria, Alberto. *Política y cultura popular: la Argentina peronista 1946–1955*. Buenos Aires: Ediciones de la Flor, 1983.

Cortázar, Julio. *Salvo el crepúsculo*. Buenos Aires: Alfaguara, 1984.

——. *Los premios*. Buenos Aires: Sudamericana, 1970.

——. *Último round*. Vol. II. Madrid: Siglo XXI, 1974.

——. *La vuelta al día en ochenta mundos*. México, D. F.: Siglo XXI, 1967.

——. *Obra crítica*. 3 vols. Madrid: Alfaguara, 1994.

Lewis, Martin A. *Afro-Argentine Discourse: Another Dimension of the Black Diaspora*. Columbia: University of Missouri Press, 1996.

Martínez, Tomás Eloy. *Las memorias del General*. Buenos Aires: Planeta, 1996.

Matamoro, Blas. *Diccionario privado de Jorge Luis Borges*. Madrid: Altalena, 1979.

Naipaul, V. S. *The Return of Eva Perón*. New York: Knopf, 1980.

Page, Joseph A. *Perón: A Biography*. New York: Random House,1983.

Sebreli, Juan José. *Los deseos imaginarios del peronismo*. Buenos Aires: Sudamericana, 1992.

Tedesco, Luis O. *Cancionero de Enrique S. Discépolo*. Buenos Aires: Torres Agüero, 1977.

——. *Cancionero de José González Castillo y Cátulo Castillo*. Buenos Aires: Torres Agüero, 1977.

——. *Cancionero de Enrique Cadícamo*. Buenos Aires: Torres Agüero, 1977.

De la investigación periodística al *potin*: El relato documental argentino de fin de siglo

Hugo Hortiguera

[L]as cuestiones impersonales sólo suscitan nuestro interés cuando las enfocamos – equivocadamente – bajo un ángulo personalizado.
(Lipovetsky 64)

Como bien señalan Ford y Longo, un fenómeno notable de la cultura argentina en las últimas décadas parece ser un incremento de la articulación narrativa de la información, en lugar de presentar una forma macroestructural de discurso informativo-argumentativo (131).[1] Siempre según estos autores, esta nueva forma de *non-fiction* se caracterizaría por un desdibujamiento de los límites entre lo público y lo privado, y entre la información y la narración, con recursos prestados, muchas veces, de la ficción. Este hecho llevaría a provocar una zona ambigua que se debatiría siempre entre estas dos imposibilidades: la de presentarse como una ficción – puesto que los hechos ocurrieron y el lector es consciente de ello – y la de intentar ser un "fiel" reflejo de los acontecimientos.

La ingerencia cada vez mayor de los medios y otros sistemas de control social sobre lo privado buscaría, por una parte, reforzar la credibilidad de éstos mediante una información individualizada y "constatable". Por otro lado, los cruces cada vez más obvios entre información y procedimientos propios de la narrativa podrían tener su causa en la permanente desconfianza discursiva que ha existido históricamente en la cultura argentina. Este hecho traería consigo, cada vez más, una mayor sospecha de los discursos argumentativos de las llamadas "zonas duras de los medios" (Ford y Longo 132).

En el presente estudio, nos proponemos describir cómo esta relación entre lo ficcional y lo "real" parece tensarse en la Argentina de fines de siglo, creando un tipo discursivo que, escrito la mayor parte por periodistas, pareciera deconstruir, muchas veces, estas categorías. Analizaremos entonces cómo se constituyen los sistemas de representación que construyen este "real", creando un espacio intersticial en donde se funden todos los límites genéricos, y al que llamaremos, a falta de mejor nombre, el relato documental argentino de fin de siglo.

Queremos aclarar, sin embargo, que, si bien en una primera aproximación este tipo de relatos pareciera compartir algunas prácticas propias del testimonio (sobre todo en aquellos aspectos ejemplarizantes o denunciatorios), se diferencia de aquél en algunos elementos básicos. En primer lugar, aunque sus autores son periodistas, no tiene por fin contar la historia de las voces subalternas, sino más bien desenmascarar la apropiación patrimonialista del Estado y las prácticas de silencios y encubrimientos que han hecho aquéllos que han formado parte del poder político y económico del país durante los años noventa. Esta es, quizás, una diferencia esencial. No es la incorporación en el espacio letrado de aquéllos que no lo son gracias a la intermediación de un "letrado solidario", como lo llama Achugar (56), sino de un crítico que se "separa" de su(s) figura(s) y de los acontecimientos que narra. Este narrador pondrá en evidencia las manipulaciones de estas personalidades públicas a partir de algunos informantes anónimos (generalmente muy allegados al poder) que le transmitirán, "en confianza" y en contrapunto, otras versiones e interpretaciones de las aparecidas en el discurso oficial.

En segundo lugar, en algunos casos, pueden aparecer como textos "oportunistas", en el sentido de que aprovechan la inmediatez de los acontecimientos públicos, recurriendo, algunas veces, al rumor, el chisme y la crónica del espectáculo. Esto último resulta destacable, ya que aquello mismo que critican (la farandulización o espectacularización de la vida política) terminaría convirtiéndose en algunos de ellos en uno de los ingredientes de este discurso, acompañado casi siempre por cierto componente "escandaloso".

En tercer lugar, estos textos parecieran bordear una frontera borrosa respecto a su intención. Por un lado, intentarían producir un cambio de conciencia – con un fin más didáctico, si se quiere –. Y así lo aclaran, muchas veces, en sus prólogos, solapas y cubiertas. Por otro, en sus casos más extremos, jugarían con componentes de divertimento o entretenimiento, al glosar la tragedia política mediante recursos robados del melodrama u otros subgéneros literarios.[2]

Por último, su cruce con el ensayo no puede obviarse. Según Sheines, el ensayo es, quizás, la forma literaria propiamente argentina. Este hecho sería un elemento básico que diferenciaría la narrativa argentina del resto de la latinoamericana: las novelas argentinas serían, para esta autora, ensayos que se esconden detrás de una apariencia novelística. La insistencia en este género por parte de nuestros autores habría impedido que se incorporaran en nuestra literatura lo real maravilloso característico de otras latitudes latinoamericanas. Y aunque en algunos ejemplos (como en el caso de *Los perros del paraíso*, *La reina del Plata* o *Copyright*) los juegos verbales parecieran emparentarla con la literatura latinoamericana "clásica", la semejanza es solamente superficial, ya que debajo de todas ellas se encontraría un sustrato ensayístico. Este puede detectarse en los insistentes cuestionamientos sobre la identidad, el fracaso, el pasado o la prehistoria nacional. También puede reconocerse en el planteamiento de una tesis, en la manera de sus formulaciones, en sus aproximaciones conceptuales. "Pero el ensayo también es una actitud, una manera de vivir, de gobernar, de hacer. Y como tal es el meollo de la conducta de muchos argentinos" (Sheines 134).

Hechas estas salvedades entonces, prestaremos especial atención a cómo muchos de los aspectos que mencionábamos más arriba producen relatos que parecieran ir evolucionando cada vez más hacia lo que, en el ámbito francés se reconoce como *potin*, entendiendo por esto una forma discursiva periodística en la cual "quelqu'un (l'auteur, le narrateur) parle à un autre (le lecteur) d'une personne absente dans un but plus ou moins avoué de communiquer une information –ou pseudo-information– négative ou tendancieuse concernant celui-ci, sans présenter d'arguments décisifs" (Van Den Heuvel 192) y definido por el *Robert* como "Bavardage, commérage; chronique mondaine, plus ou moins scandaleuse; petites médisances" (citado por Van Den Heuvel 193).

En el presente ensayo, tomaremos como textos de referencia algunos de los llamados "trabajos de investigación periodística" producidos durante la década de los noventa acerca del gobierno del Dr. Carlos Menem. En especial, intentaremos ejemplificar con los espacios paratextuales de muchos de estos trabajos, habida cuenta de que en ellos es observable una particular condensación semántica y su estudio detallado nos ofrece una muestra concentrada y compendiada de lo que los textos completos nos brindan en mayor escala.

De lo público a lo privado: la serie Menem

Cualquiera que visitara alguna librería argentina durante la última década del siglo XX, se encontraría con mesas enteras de libros dedicados a la llamada "investigación periodística", textos que, desde diversos ángulos, intentaban dar cuenta del fenómeno menemista. La figura del entonces presidente ocupará un lugar destacado en la escritura argentina y algunos aspectos de su vida (pública y privada) serán narrativizados casi melodramáticamente. Tampoco se olvidarán de otros personajes ligados a él en forma directa o indirecta y con quienes también se seguirá un procedimiento similar. (Obsérvese el carácter metonímico de estas figuras: el relato de la vida pública y privada de estos personajes se convierte en representativo del poder político y económico del país.)

En 1991, a casi dos años de la asunción del Dr. Menem, Horacio Verbitsky inaugura con su *Robo para la corona. Los frutos prohibidos del árbol de la corrupción* toda una serie discursiva que marcará los años noventa en Argentina. Por un lado, introduce temáticamente el "caso Menem" y las complicidades y corruptelas entre el empresariado local y los políticos. Por otro, mediante el cruce de los saberes legales y económicos con información salida desde dentro mismo del poder político, se intentará describir la base sobre la que se construirá la Argentina de los años siguientes.

Hay que hacer, sin embargo, una salvedad. En el ejemplo concreto de Verbitsky, no se toma tan abiertamente el retrato *privado* de Menem como eje estructurador del relato (como sí lo harán otros textos posteriores), sino que se relatan en detalle los manejos turbios de sus acciones públicas y sus consecuencias políticas y económicas en los primeros meses de su gobierno. Las acciones políticas del presidente argentino y sus allegados circulan por sus páginas en todo momento, desnudando el tráfico de influencias que se comenzará a manifestar descaradamente por entonces. En textos subsiguientes, mientras tanto, se explotará la vida íntima de los implicados y el sentido de la inmediatez, recurriendo a acontecimientos muy recientes y conocidos por el público lector nacional.[3]

En varios de estos textos, ya en el título mismo, se plantean fenómenos de transposición y cruces con otras formas discursivas (para el concepto de transposición ver Steimberg 16). Así, el relato de suspenso, el policial, el melodrama, junto con la biografía, el relato de "chismes del espectáculo" y hasta lo grotesco coexistirán en muchos de ellos, apelando a mecanismos intertextuales que se alimentan, muchas veces, de otros medios audiovisuales (reportajes televisivos, radiales, revistas del espectáculo, inclusión de fotografías). De esta manera, se apela a un corpus de variantes genéricas y estilísticas que no terminan por unificarse y que friccionan en el interior de la diégesis, provocando continuas contaminaciones con modelos, fórmulas o dispositivos literarios y periodísticos de larga tradición. Esta modalidad intertextual es observable, en el libro de Verbitsky, en la titulación de algunos de sus capítulos, que abrevan en una terminología propia de la ficción ("Argumento", "Personajes") o en relaciones de intertitularidad con obras famosas ("Moby Dick", "Los diamantes son eternos"), pero también por su título y subtítulo.

En notable alusión a una frase adjudicada a un ministro del gobierno menemista (José Luis Manzano), el título en cuestión de Verbitsky (*Robo para la corona*) pareciera aludir a una supuesta novela de aventuras. Con una obvia ausencia de imágenes en el diseño de tapa, el subtítulo, en tanto, (*Los frutos prohibidos del árbol de la corrupción*) propondría conexiones bíblicas ("los frutos prohibidos del Edén"), al tiempo que establecería un anclaje con la realidad política y económica circundante del país, pero también encubriría una ironía que juega con el apellido del ministro que dijera esa frase: *Manzano* – frutos prohibidos – *árbol* de la corrupción. La contratapa y el prólogo (diferenciado del resto del texto mediante letra cursiva), en tanto, anticipan un estudio periodístico que, confiesa, tiene por fin darle al lector las herramientas indispensables para poder entender el funcionamiento de la legalidad administrativa durante el primer gobierno del Dr. Menem, dejando de lado el relato de lo humano o la peripecia personal e íntima (Verbitsky 10).

El espectáculo del/en el vestíbulo: la palabra desplazada

Otros textos producidos más tarde, por su parte, explotarán en sus espacios paratextuales este cruce con otras series – la literaria "consagrada", la folletinesca y hasta la histórica –, a la vez que insistirán en un sentido del espectáculo que se acrecentará a medida que nos adentramos en los noventa. Basta recorrer los índices de algunos de ellos, para confirmar lo que venimos diciendo: "La malquerida del harem", "La Lolita musulmana", "El joven Casanova del subdesarrollo", "La princesa de Nonogasta" (*Pizza con champán*); "Divórciate y anda", "El Rey Sol", "Años de rojo carmesí" (*Menem. La vida privada*); "Drama en Byscaine Point Circle", "Viaje a la superficie del harem", "Si quiere tener otro hijo, yo me mato", "Un choque de rubias", "Dicen los astros: 'No habrá boda'" (*Cecilia querida*).

Las portadas, por otra parte, parecen evolucionar de forma similar. Si con Verbitsky (Fig. 1) todavía queda espacio para recuperar y recentrar una palabra dicha entre bambalinas (la infeliz frase del ministro Manzano puesta en tapa, en título catástrofe, con fondo uniforme y sin fotografías que distraigan la atención del lector), las cubiertas siguientes de la "serie Menem" comienzan a desplazarla.[4] Así, la imagen comienza a ocupar cada vez mayor relevancia y la palabra, funcionando como "soporte" de ella, empieza a marginalizarse, a relegarse, o a cumplir función de "relleno". Tal es el caso, tal vez, de *El jefe* de Cerruti.

Publicada por Planeta en 1993, la tapa de Cerruti presenta texto e ilustración ocupando la portada en partes iguales, con un marcado eje vertical que provoca un efecto de mayor dinamismo (Fig. 2). Se ofrece en ella, mediante una foto en blanco y negro, el perfil recortado de Menem enfrentado al título, dispuesto en forma vertical en la mitad izquierda de la página. Como bien señala Vázquez respecto de este trabajo periodístico, el perfil elegido del político ha sido el de una estatuaria casi romana: "en los rasgos simiescos del hombre que allí se ve, en la dureza de sus formas, se intuye una férrea voluntad de poder" (193). Con la mirada de Menem hacia la izquierda, se produce un efecto fotográfico más dinámico. Su único ojo visible, ubicado en uno de los centros de interés de la página, mira con firmeza y ambición hacia la palabra "jefe", colocada desproporcionadamente frente a él. Y al aludir, con su subtítulo, a una vida y obra que merece ser relatada y leída, se lo inscribe en la Historia.

Seis años más tarde, en la investigación de Olga Wornat, *Menem. La vida privada* (Fig. 3), se muestra un tres cuartos de perfil que queda encerrado, muy teatralmente, entre el título y subtítulo (éste último, curiosamente, tapándole la boca). Con un rostro que parece perder su mirada en regiones superiores, la imagen de Menem pareciera buscar la cima de los sentimientos elevados, alejada de cualquier contradicción mundana. La diagramación, así, divide el espacio en tres partes, siendo la más importante la fotografía del entonces presidente, aparentemente extraída de una escena televisiva. Este hecho no debiera pasar inadvertido. Imponiéndose entre las palabras por su sola presencia, sus labios aparecen sellados por una "vida privada" que coquetea, en todo momento, con la exposición abierta y descarada en los medios.

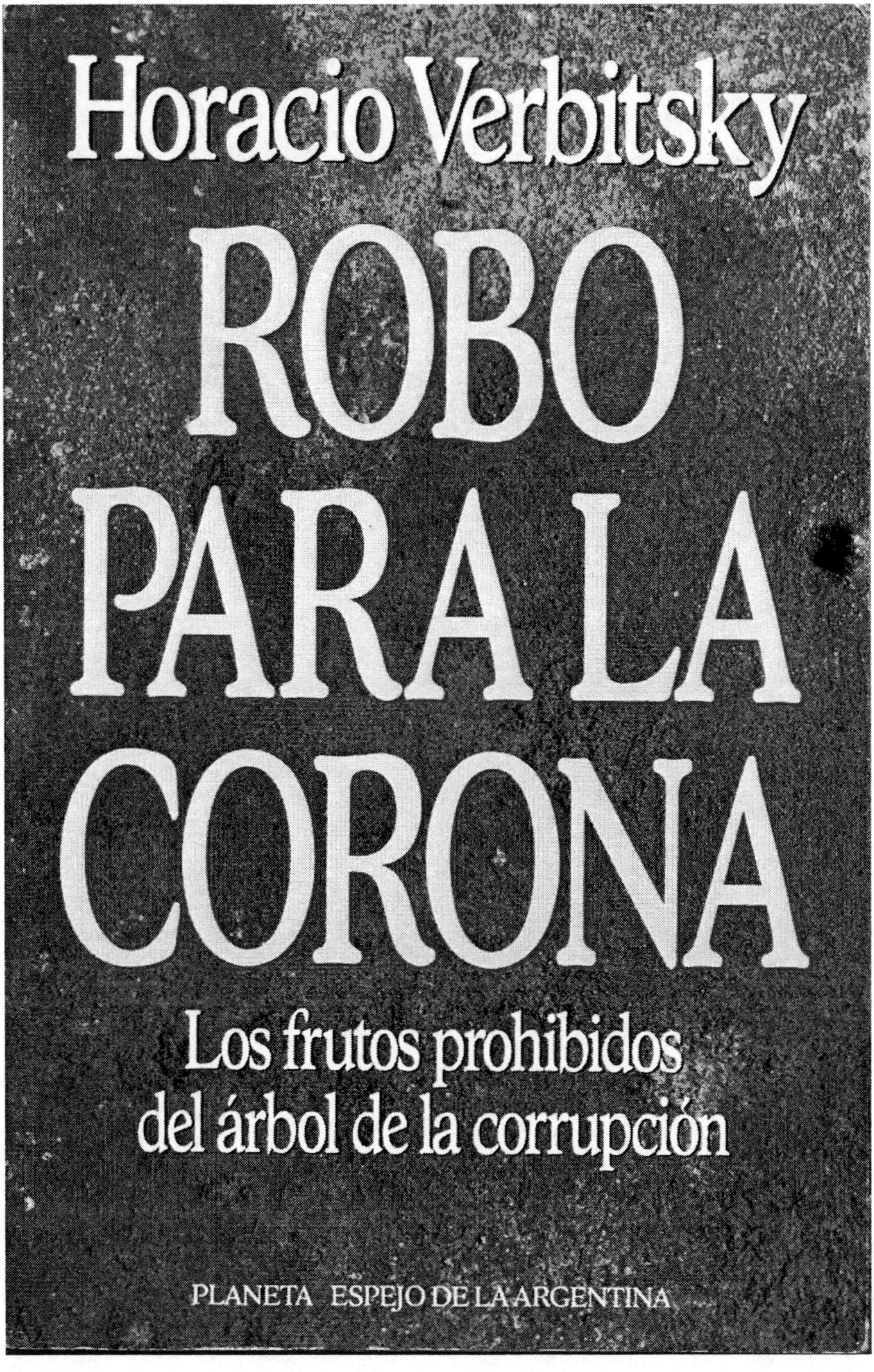

Horacio Verbitsky

ROBO PARA LA CORONA

Los frutos prohibidos del árbol de la corrupción

PLANETA ESPEJO DE LA ARGENTINA

Figure 1

Figure 2

102.000 ejemplares vendidos

MENEM

LA VIDA PRIVADA

Olga Wornat

Prólogo de Sylvina Walger

Planeta

Figure 3

Si en aquel texto de Cerruti de 1993 subyacía, según Vázquez (193), una intencionalidad histórica ("la imagen de un político que se quería prócer"), un sexenio más tarde se excluía todo sistema de representación del poder, con el fin de mostrar la parte privada e íntima del presidente, su afán "farandulero", su exposición mediática. Una y otra tapa, uno y otro texto, desnudan un cambio ideológico fundamental que va de la separación de la vida del político y su obra y la exhibición de una "vida ejemplar" digna de memoria (recuérdese el subtítulo de Cerruti: *Vida y obra de Carlos Saúl Menem*), a la imposibilidad de establecer ámbitos separados para las actividades privadas del hombre Menem y los asuntos del Estado. El texto de Wornat, en efecto, explorará estas relaciones siempre confusas y ambiguas que durante su presidencia se establecieron entre la vida privada y la pública del político. Será a través de lo privado que podrá entenderse lo público, poniendo en evidencia así una práctica discursiva hipócrita que ha terminado por equiparar delito y poder como contracaras de una misma moneda.

El espectáculo de la imagen

En otros textos posteriores, las imágenes desplazan cada vez más las palabras hacia los márgenes o juegan con ellas como simples actos decorativos. Al colocarse los rostros de los políticos en el centro, pareciera reproducirse la forma en que éstos incursionan en el espacio audiovisual de fin de siglo. De esta manera, se desnuda un fenómeno de espectacularización de lo político que se manifestará singularmente durante los noventa, y que traerá consigo "modificaciones serias que se dan tanto en el nivel del discurso como en los cambios que se experimentan al pasar del predominio de la cultura letrada a la cultura audiovisual" (Quevedo 206).

Éste es el caso de *Menem-Bolocco S.A.* (de Wornat, otra vez) y *Cecilia querida. Historia de un amor improbable* (de Rodríguez Villouta).[5] Lo interesante en el diseño del primero de ellos (Fig. 4) son los múltiples signos que se deslizan no tan inocentemente en la ilustración de tapa (el signo "pesos" recorriendo toda la decoración del pastel, los muñequitos de boda casi caricaturescos y autistas en su piso superior). El mensaje verbal que acompaña al dibujo, asimismo, termina anclando y orientando las imágenes hacia una insinuación de una boda "por conveniencia" (el "S.A" agregado al final).

Por otra parte, en el juego de tapa y contratapa (Fig. 5), anverso y reverso, parecería anunciarse una intención de contar "el detrás de la escena", anticipando, mediante una puesta kitsch, ciertas revelaciones escandalosas de la vida privada de uno de los hombres públicos más famosos de la Argentina.[6] Estos ecos kitsch se aprecian en el uso de las iniciales ornamentadas en el título, que intenta reproducir, por otra parte, una tipografía característica de las invitaciones de bodas; en el color amarillo de las letras, que evoca cierto efecto "dorado"; en el fondo rojo, viejo cliché evocador de la pasión; en la línea decorativa con muchas inflexiones y pocos cortes que, a manera de

Figure 4

Figure 5

fileteado, subraya el "S.A" del título; en fin, en toda la decoración del pastel, con sus rosetones, frenesí por el abigarramiento y ornamentación a ultranza. Los nombres de los involucrados, a su vez, puestos en tapa y sin ningún otro comentario, terminan funcionando como otro anzuelo que servirá para acrecentar el interés por el texto y despertar la curiosidad de cierto público lector habituado al *potin*, y cuyo placer pareciera residir en un discurso de evasión (cf. Van Den Heuvel 218). Desde esta perspectiva, la inclusión de fotografías en su interior podría cumplir la función de las típicas ilustraciones que se pueden encontrar en este tipo de publicaciones. No podemos obviar, por último, el oportunismo de la edición: el libro apareció en las librerías argentinas el mismo fin de semana en el que el ex-presidente se casara.

Por otro lado, además de estos guiños con respecto a este producto periodístico particular, parecieran cruzarse referencias tanto al folletín como a la novela rosa.[7] Mientras la ilustración se centra nada menos que en la boda – secuencia final de toda novela rosa que se precie –, la solapa redobla aquella alusión. En efecto, se instaura en ella una ampulosidad que se regodea en una polifonía de signos, en una retórica de excesos que recurre al diálogo melodramático (reproduciendo las primeras líneas del texto) y al suspenso.

El uso de la "oralidad", pero también de la repetición, aparece aquí – en solapa y, más tarde, en su interior – de manera mucho más marcada y "melodramatizada" que en textos precedentes:

> Te juro, Nena, que ella no durmió en Olivos, no pasó nada... Te lo juro por la memoria de Carlitos... Creeme, por favor... –dijo Carlos Menem con desesperación. Del otro lado del teléfono su hija sollozaba y, entre ahogos, amenazaba con dejar de verlo para siempre si la historia entre Cecilia Bolocco y él, que los medios insinuaban, era verdadera. (solapa)

La escena propia de una novelita rosa con la que se abre el primer capítulo será reproducida y adelantada en la solapa con pequeñísimas modificaciones, añadiendo los típicos clichés de este tipo de composiciones: los amores contrariados, las pasiones desenfrenadas y las "vidas miserables" de los ricos y famosos. Asimismo, la apertura de la solapa, con ese diálogo que reproducimos más arriba, adelanta otro componente importante del texto. Relato frívolo, *potin* y ficción melodramatizada encubierta bajo la apariencia de un trabajo de investigación periodística, lo que dominará en su diégesis será un universo de hablas, de citaciones, una dinámica de discursos engendrada por una dialéctica conversacional, una mezcla de instancias de enunciación: las voces de las figuras públicas y los textos periodísticos citados por Wornat tantas veces, pero también los comentarios y alusiones que, a veces, socarronamente, ésta hará de ellos.

En el estilo de Wornat se aprecia una recurrente clave irónica, notable, por ejemplo, en las frases breves resumidoras que cierran algunos párrafos. Por ejemplo, después de describir las ambiciones similares del dúo Menem-Bolocco ("Amaban la fama y el poder. Los lujos, el dinero y los escándalos.

Los sahumerios orientales y las velas perfumadas. La meditación, las cartas astrales y el control mental"), concluye: "Dos auténticas almas gemelas" (18). Luego de describir los "consejos de vida" dados por Bolocco a quien quisiera escucharla, acota: "Una auténtica predicadora" (57). Después de comentar las preferencias lectoras de ésta por Paulo Coelho, sintetiza: "Era una auténtica chica zen" (70).

Con un claro objetivo publicitario y comercial, desde el espacio paratextual se produce, además, una intervención que indica cómo debe leerse el texto que sigue. En efecto, a la reiteración de este supuesto diálogo entre el presidente y su hija, le sigue una (auto)declaración que reacomoda el texto en fronteras genéricas muy borrosas, al tiempo que se ubica en su relación con otro texto previo de su autora y se declara como verdadero fenómeno de ventas.

De esta manera, la solapa juega con elementos que ubican el libro en un espacio ambiguo y mestizo. En él se cruzan la investigación periodística ("implacable investigación y el estilo periodístico descarnado"), en sintonía con otras "formas de escritura": la novela rosa ("revela los entretelones de este romance"), la de suspenso e intriga ("el poder, los negocios, la ambición y las intrigas se mezclan en un cóctel explosivo"), la biografía ("La verdadera historia de Cecilia 'Chechi' Bolocco"; "Carlos Menem, de Anillaco a la Casa Rosada y después: un viaje tormentoso"), el *potin* o relato chismoso ("Él y sus amores: ¿del harén al Edén?", "Ella y sus amores: de las cenizas a los diamantes"). Al mismo tiempo, se cierra la pequeña reseña con un cuasi *slogan* publicitario que coloca a la autora en una posición de absoluta autoridad en el tema, capaz de desnudar los secretos más obscuros de las figuras públicas ("Todos los secretos, expuestos por la única autora para quien no hay secretos"). Mientras tanto, la solapa posterior, con un claro objetivo de reforzar el sema "autoridad de la periodista", destaca su perfil profesional con un breve curriculum: su participación, como corresponsal, en la invasión estadounidense a Panamá; en las guerras de Centroamérica, Líbano y Yugoslavia; en los conflictos entre árabes e israelíes y entre Perú y Ecuador. Este perfil también se completa con su colaboración en revistas y periódicos muy populares o frívolos de Argentina (*Somos* y *Gente*), España (*Interviú*) y Chile (*La Tercera*), entre otros.

Ya en su interior, el prólogo reitera algunos de los conceptos introducidos en su solapa, estableciendo una vez más un pacto de lectura que sienta sus bases en la indefinición genérica. ¿"Realidad", "jugoso culebrón", "rompecabezas amoroso" o "(absurda) historia"? se cuestiona. Y por supuesto, no faltan los interrogantes melodramáticos que mantienen la expectativa e interés del lector y que permitirán el desarrollo de la historia:

> ¿Está [Menem] enamorado de Cecilia? ¿Qué los llevó a estar juntos y a mostrarse ostentosamente? ¿Qué hay detrás de la cándida Cecilia Bolocco? ¿Cuáles son sus secretos y por qué su desesperación por casarse con un hombre que podría ser su padre? ¿Qué ganó cada uno con este promocionado

romance? Son algunas de las preguntas que me hice mientras escribía esta historia. (10)

No podemos dejar pasar por alto la frecuencia con la que este recurso se reitera en el interior del texto. Además de su relación con la novelita rosa, las preguntas también pueden asociarse con la lógica del *potin*. En efecto, lo implícito en ellas coincide con las presuposiciones del lector y con las preguntas que él mismo se hace frente a los acontecimientos públicos. En aquellas preguntas que quedan sin respuesta directa, el lector se identifica y termina por confirmar sus sospechas. De esta manera, y mediante mecanismos indirectos, la periodista no sólo se evita cualquier juicio por difamación que pudiera sobrevenir como consecuencia de sus dichos, sino también se permite jugar con la expectativa y el placer del lector, al reconocer su propia presencia en el discurso. Como ya hemos dicho en otra oportunidad, el *potin* no sigue un esquema de texto periodístico informativo en sentido clásico, en donde se desarrolla una argumentación. En su caso, como señala Van Den Heuvel (209), no hay nada. No existe una lógica del relato, ni retórica argumentativa en la acepción estricta del término, sino un flirteo constante con la *simulación* (Van Den Heuvel 214).

En la declaración de parte de sus fuentes que se desliza como agradecimiento final en su prólogo (revistas del corazón y periódicos de Argentina y Chile, el Archivo de la Biblioteca Nacional de Santiago, de la Escuela de Periodismo de la Universidad de Chile, entre otros), además de traslucir la mezcla indiscriminada de la que el libro hará gala, le permitirá (auto)ubicarse como eslabón de una cadena discursiva, como discurso repetido que retoma y reitera lo ya dicho en distintas fuentes. La actividad receptora de la narradora (como escucha y como lectora) se revela en este cruce de voces. Pero no es ésta pasiva frente a la información que reproduce. Los comentarios irónicos, disimulados detrás del uso de las comillas o de los intentos por recrear la pronunciación riojana del presidente: "¿Miedo *io*? [...] *Io* no tengo miedo a nadie", introducen una distancia crítica que se mofa indirectamente de los involucrados (40; énfasis nuestro).

Lo significativo en este texto está dado, entonces, por los desvíos que toma la periodista en presentar su punto de vista, en los mecanismos indirectos a los que acude para decir "su palabra". En este sentido, el mestizaje genérico se convierte en elemento fundamental. Toda la actividad escrituraria pareciera dirigirse hacia un reencuentro de discursos que conviven en un mismo espacio textual, caracterizado por una ausencia de límites, por una ostentación discursiva que pareciera anular la visibilidad del emisor. Sin embargo, detrás de esta exhibición de voces se disimularía, en verdad, la suya propia. A diferencia del *potin* clásico, en donde se tiende a la despersonalización de la palabra del emisor, en donde se anulan las distancias entre emisor y receptor (Van Den Heuvel 214), el texto de Wornat, como vemos, se ríe de esta convención y la retuerce. Así, al introducir, ladinamente, un distanciamiento irónico, no haría más que explotar las verdaderas connotaciones del discurso vacuo de los involucrados, con sus lugares comunes, y el de la prensa cómplice encargada de reproducirlo.

En definitiva, la recurrencia al formato del *potin* aquí no haría más que dramatizar un discurso hueco y vacío que se disfraza con una retórica de imágenes y espejos detrás de la cual no hay nada. Vale decir, el texto parodia esa práctica discursiva hipócrita y llena su diégesis con una dinámica de saturación (de diálogos, de imágenes fotográficas, de voces que se cruzan, de referencias a otros géneros literarios no prestigiosos). En fin, se construye un espacio como modelo de la abundancia que esconde, paradójicamente, una carencia.

El romance de la bella y la bestia

Por la misma fecha en que se edita el libro de Wornat, y aprovechando el reciente casamiento de Menem con Cecilia Bolocco, la chilena Mili Rodríguez Villouta publica *Cecilia querida. Historia de un amor improbable* (2001). Entre ambos textos parece establecerse una red de elementos en común: el oportunismo de su aparición (los dos textos aparecen en las librerías porteñas casi simultáneamente el mismo fin de semana en que se produce la boda del ex-presidente argentino), la similitud en el diseño de su presentación y su redacción. Sin embargo, en esta otra parecen intensificarse y exagerarse algunos motivos, en un juego exhibicionista que apuntaría a un "desmadre" espectacular de signos (Lipovetsky 171).

Entre los rostros sonrientes de Menem y Bolocco en fondo de terciopleo rojo, serpentea, como en un arabesco, el nombre de la autora y el título, en el que parecen conjugarse dos emisores diferentes (Fig. 6). En efecto, al *Cecilia querida*, posiblemente una frase dicha por el propio Menem a su reciente esposa, se le agrega el subtítulo *Historia de un amor improbable*, juicio valorativo que podría ser adjudicado a la autora y que de entrada determina su posición enunciativa.[8] El texto fija la cadena flotante de los significados que la imagen edulcorada de la pareja intenta transmitir. Junto con el supuesto discurso amoroso de sus miradas alambicadas y la frase afectuosa que, como diálogo fotonovelesco, se interpone entre los dos personajes, se incorpora la insinuación y la sospecha de un discurso falso: el amor improbable de los protagonistas. En definitiva, en esta mezcla de lo visual con lo verbal se comprime liminarmente todo el libro, atrayendo la atención del lector en una lectura que pone en evidencia el simulacro discursivo, la mentira de la imagen y su puesta en escena.

En la síntesis que se anticipa en la contratapa, por otra parte, se describe un contenido cargado de clichés y convencionalismos: amantes ricos, famosos y furtivos, *resort* en Miami, mar turquesa, *paparazzis* ambiciosos, cóctel de *glamour* y *thriller* peligroso, el poder y la belleza, las presiones políticas,

Figure 6

los intereses económicos y los conceptos morales. En su exagerada retórica kitsh, con la saturación de vocablos extranjeros que denotan sofisticación, sus guiños encubiertos al teatro – "el amor que une al político con *la bella dama de los ensueños*" (el subrayado nos pertenece) – y su promesa de situaciones conflictivas, el texto exaspera hiperbólicamente las relaciones entre lo teatral y lo político, mientras que subraya el abismo y artificio que desde el poder se crea entre imagen y realidad para obtener un efecto emocional. En una palabra, aparecerían desenmascarados la teatralidad de la vida privada del político, su puesta en escena, su falta de sinceridad, sus sentimientos falsos y, una vez más, su simulación (Schwartzenberg 111).

Por otra parte, mediante la saturación de convencionalismos en el paratexto (con sus alusiones a la riqueza, fama y edad de los protagonistas; ambiente fastuoso; conflictos varios y enrevesados; con su correspondiente misterio, ritmo dinámico y ágil de la narración y suspenso final), Rodríguez Villouta pareciera terminar por provocar un efecto que, por su exageración, se acerca a lo caricaturesco o farsesco. Más tarde, se verá cómo la estrategia de tapa y contratapa se reiterará en el interior del texto. Así, mientras el fotomontaje de portada, con la yuxtaposición de los personajes famosos involucrados y la distancia gráfica que los separa mantiene la incertidumbre, y el adjetivo "improbable" anticipa, paradójicamente, una supuesta investigación sobre un amor imposible de probar, los capítulos de *Cecilia querida* continuarán con esa irresolución y ambigüedad.

De esta manera, el discurso se dirige al lector como un murmullo de múltiples voces, de citas estereotipadas que no dicen nada que no se haya dicho o leído ya antes. "Two clichés make us laugh but a hundred clichés move us because we sense dimly that the clichés are talking among themselves, celebrating a reunion" (Eco 209). Como ejemplo, la mayoría de los títulos de los capítulos hace referencia a frases dichas por los involucrados, entrecomilladas o no, que eclosionan entre sí y que evocan, a su vez, diálogos folletinescos o periodísticos: "Papi no se casa"; "Lo vi con mis propios ojos"; "Vamos a tal lugar, pero tú tómate un avión y yo otro"; "No está enamorado de mí"; "No te preocupes mi amor"; "Si quiere tener otro hijo, yo me mato"; "¡No sé si me caso!"; "¡Sacáme de aquí!"; "Hoy un reportaje con ella cuesta 15 mil dólares".

Este efecto repetitivo es uno de los más obvios de todo el texto. En su recurrencia a la novelita rosa, por ejemplo, reproducirá un diálogo de Karina Lafontaine, personaje interpretado por Bolocco en el teleteatro *Morelia*, plagado de lugares comunes (29). Una página más tarde, repetirá el gesto, pero para describir una situación de la vida real entre Bolocco y su primer esposo: "Y cuando Michael llegó, ella salió corriendo a saludarlo a la puerta y *le dio un beso con pierna levantada para darle más dramatismo*" (31. El subrayado es nuestro.).

Se provoca, así, un efecto redundante. Se ejecuta un juego de malabarismos con la información, hablando sobre lo ya conocido, sobre declaraciones ya leídas en innumerables revistas sensacionalistas que a veces necesitan ser "traducidas": Zulemita, la hija de Menem, "no se sostenía en pie. Se desmayó en el departamento de su madre ('cayó al suelo con unos jeans y una t-shirt Dolce & Gabanna', detalló una publicación)" (47). En esta repetición, los signos terminan autorrepresentándose. Se autodesignan, se vuelcan sobre sí, siguiendo un proceso de tipo humorístico que se burla de sí mismo (Lipovetsky 152). Por otra parte, el uso exasperado de clichés y evocaciones más reconocibles permitiría poner en escena un código que se desnaturalizaría, al llevar al lector a prestar más atención a la convención que al relato en sí.

Asimismo, también se cruzan evocaciones y guiños con otros textos de la serie Menem: con *Menem. La vida privada*, de Wornat (56), con *Pizza con champán*, de Walger (42), el *Menem-Bolocco S.A.*, de Wornat otra vez (162). Es interesante ver también cómo el texto juega siempre con el concepto de una fachada que parodia a otra. En efecto, son notables las comparaciones hiperbólicas que se hacen de estas figuras y sus conductas, casi siempre con otras propias de la realeza europea o del *jet set* norteamericano. Así, el texto reproducirá declaraciones de entrevistados que asociarán a Bolocco con "una princesa" (21), "una emperatriz" (21), "la reina del Santiago College" (79) y de "la televisión chilena" (104), con "aire de *Dinastía* pasado de moda" (124), "lo más parecido a Lady Di" (127), la "Jacqueline Onassis a escala" (229) y compararán su primera boda como "inspirada en las realezas europeas, a escala chilena" (22). Zulemita Yoma, en tanto, será la "princesa argentina", la "Diana argentina", mientras que Menem aparecerá como "el galán" (56), "el actor" (58), "John Travolta" (61).

En la inundación de citas o en la reiteración de declaraciones, disfrazada detrás de la supuesta objetividad de la información, "como si existiera un REAL de la actualidad que los medios, retroactivamente, reproducen más o menos bien" (Verón 31), la narración hace evidente que no existe más que representación, y que, fuera de ella, no se representa nada más (Block de Behar 152). Es llamativo, en este sentido, el uso frecuente de los "se dice", que, además de omitir al agente productor de la emisión, incorporan la voz anónima del público al introducir una identificación entre la curiosidad de éste y las sospechas sugeridas ladinamente por la periodista. Este procedimiento de "despersonalización" y de indentificación con el público esconde también un componente de insinuación e inmunidad personal detrás de la cual la periodista, al igual que lo hacía Wornat con su texto, se escuda.

Serán las palabras de los protagonistas y sus allegados, llenas de clichés y lugares comunes, las que importan, y Rodríguez Villouta se presentará como una costurera que irá uniendo esos retazos textuales. Escondida, sin embargo, aviesamente detrás de esos zurcidos, su voz manipulará al lector, al forzarlo a percibir la articulación de los modelos retóricos e ideológicos de producción del discurso menemista, basado siempre en imágenes, en disimulos que no representan otra cosa más allá. La palabra de/en los medios ha terminado por ser un medio que se ha transformado en un fin. En ella parece terminar y empezar todo (Block de Behar 154).

Así, el acto de leer diálogos o declaraciones será uno de los procedimientos estructuradores de todo un discurso que parece apuntar a señalar el hecho de que la realidad no es más que el discurso que la enuncia, cargado éste siempre de artificio, cita y estrategias para seducir al espectador/lector (Verón 31; Amar Sánchez 193), sin cuestionar los orígenes inciertos de la información. En definitiva, en su uso redundante, en su artificialidad, en su recurrencia al cliché, al estereotipo y a los lugares comunes, el discurso de Villouta se abisma, conjugando en él mismo aquello que se propone denunciar en la discursividad del político: si no una puesta en escena, al menos una "puesta en ficción" (Block de Behar 97).

A modo de breve conclusión

En el desarrollo de nuestro trabajo, intentamos un acercamiento al "relato documental argentino de fin de siglo" escrito sobre el período de Menem. En él, hemos visto cómo su manifestación más evidente radica en el hecho de que las formas argumentativas y críticas dan paso al goce de un espectáculo *per se*. La forma narrativa se caracteriza por una simple acumulación de anécdotas en donde, además, se neutralizarían límites y bordes genéricos.

En el ensamblaje de códigos varios, en la confusión de límites entre el folletín, la novela rosa, el *thriller*, el relato periodístico, el reportaje, el rumor o el chisme parece encubrirse, como en abismo, una estrategia que no hace más que reflejar otra que se esconde detrás del discurso político. La multiplicidad menemista solamente puede entenderse a partir de una miríada de códigos que resaltan su artificio, que destacan su desconocimiento de la distinción entre lo serio y lo frívolo, que se juega en los bordes.

Este borroneo de límites, esta *vacilación* que ha permitido una invasión de lo privado en lo público, ha llevado a una *violación* no sólo de normas legales, sino también culturales. Así, si desde el campo político de los noventa, como ha señalado Quevedo (217), se redefinía el vínculo entre medios y política, entre farandulización y poder y se legitimizaban nuevas formas de representación política (con la videopolítica, como uno de los ejemplos más notables), desde el campo periodístico/literario se responderá también con nuevas formas de narrar.

De esta manera, mientras el político argentino de fin de siglo desarrolla sus estrategias discursivas incursionando en escenarios o espacios no habituales, los textos que intentarán hablar sobre ellos reiterarán estos procedimientos. Se saturarán con emociones, con apelaciones al mundo privado, con un uso abundante del componente descriptivo – que apunta a una mayor narrativización, pero no a una argumentación estricta – y con una hibridización o aglutinación genérica casi impúdica que pareciera descuidar, en superficie, el razonamiento de los problemas.

Esta nueva escritura, con éxito desigual, se apropiará de esas estrategias, las abismará y las reflejará, desnudando en todo momento una nueva forma de acceso al fantasma de un lenguaje que termina por hacer crónica la cultura de la sospecha discursiva. En este sentido, resulta llamativo que la mayor parte de los textos estudiados intentan presentarse como "traductores" o "interpretantes" de un lenguaje de fin de siglo que hace política desde los medios, "hablando de otra cosa", encubriéndose detrás de máscaras y despolitizando el discurso político.

Por otra parte, hemos visto también que en los textos más recientes se pone un énfasis importante en la imagen que acompaña a las palabras. La presencia del *potin* es, quizás, un ejemplo notable, con sus connotaciones de discurso chismoso (que habla) "del espectáculo". Esto no es un dato menor, si se tiene en cuenta que durante estos diez años la comunicación política cedió la fuerza de la palabra (vacía de propuestas y devenida ahora en mero instrumento de adorno) a la preeminencia de la seducción de la imagen y el sentido de *show business*, en donde la forma se ha transformado en su contenido. En definitiva, una estética de abarrotamiento, desmesura y saturación, de espacio construido como modelo de abundancia obscena que enmascara, paradójicamente y con dispar resultado, un proceso de carencia, de vacío de referente, de crítica de éste y de la representación.

Obras citadas

Achugar, Hugo. "Historias paralelas/historias ejemplares: la Historia y la voz del otro." *Revista de Crítica Literaria Latinoamericana* 36 (1992): 49–71.

Aguirre Aragón, Erick. "Control discursivo y alteridad en el testimonio centroamericano. Cinco modelos representativos." *Istmo. Revista virtual de estudios literarios y culturales* 2 (2001) <http://www.wooster.edu/istmo/articulos/contro.html>

Amar Sánchez, Ana María. "Estrategias de seductores. Una política del placer." *Letrados iletrados. Apropiaciones y representaciones de lo popular en literatura.* Ed. Ana María Zubieta. Buenos Aires: Eudeba, 1999. 187–97.

Baudrillard, Jean. *Revenge of the Crystal. Selected Writings on the Modern Object and its Destiny, 1968–1983.* Sydney: Pluto Press Australia, 1990.

Block de Behar, Lisa. *Dos medios entre dos medios. Sobre la representación y sus dualidades.* Buenos Aires: Siglo Veintiuno Editores, 1990.

Bonasso, Miguel. *Don Alfredo.* Buenos Aires: Planeta, 1999.

Cerruti, Gabriela. *El jefe. Vida y obra de Carlos Saúl Menem.* Buenos Aires: Planeta, 1993.

Cortéz, Beatriz. "La verdad y otras ficciones: Visiones críticas sobre el testimonio centroamericano." *Istmo. Revista virtual de estudios literarios y culturales centroamericanos* 2 (2001) <http://www.wooster.edu/istmo/articulos/testim.html>

De Grandis, Rita. *Polémica y estrategias narrativas en América Latina. José María Arguedas, Mario Vargas Llosa, Rodolfo Walsh, Ricardo Piglia.* Buenos Aires: Beatriz Viterbo Editora, 1993.

Eco, Umberto. *Travels in Hyperreality*. London: Picador, 1987.

Ford, Aníbal, y Fernanda Longo. "La exasperación del caso. Algunos problemas que plantea la narrativización de la información de interés público." *Telenovela. Ficción popular y mutaciones culturales*. Eds. Eliseo Verón y Lucrecia Escudero Chauvel. Barcelona: Gedisa, 1997. 131–39.

Jitrik, Noé. *Historia e imaginación literaria. Las posibilidades de un género*. Buenos Aires: Biblos, 1995.

Laforgue, Jorge, ed. *Textos de y sobre Rodolfo Walsh*. Buenos Aires/Madrid: Alianza Editorial, 2000.

Lipovetsky, Gilles. *La era del vacío. Ensayos sobre el individualismo contemporáneo*. Barcelona: Anagrama, 1986.

López Echagüe, Hernán. *El otro. Una biografía política de Educardo Duhalde*. Buenos Aires: Planeta, 1996.

Mackenbach, Werner. "Realidad y ficción en el testimonio centroamericano." *Istmo. Revista virtual de estudios literarios y culturales centroamericanos* 2 (2001) <http://www.wooster.edu/istmo/articulos/realidad.html>.

Majul, Luis. *Los dueños de la Argentina. La cara oculta de los negocios*. Buenos Aires: Sudamericana, 1992.

——. *Los dueños de la Argentina II. Los secretos del verdadero poder*. Buenos Aires: Sudamericana, 1994.

——. *Los nuevos ricos de la Argentina. Tiburones al acecho*. Buenos Aires: Sudamericana, 1997.

Martínez, Tomás Eloy. "El periodismo vuelve a contar historias." *La Nación* (Suplemento de Cultura) 21 de noviembre de 2001http://www.lanacion.com.ar>.

Moles, Abraham. *El kitsch. El arte de la felicidad*. Barcelona: Ediciones Paidós, 1990.

Nagy-Zekmi, Silvia. "¿Testimonio o ficción? Actitudes académicas." *Ciberletras* 5 (2000) <http://www.lehman.cuny.edu/ciberletras>.

Pérez Cuadra, María del Carmen. "El testimonio como 'fin' y ficción." *Istmo. Revista virtual de estudios literarios y culturales centroamericanos* 2 (2001) <http://www.wooster.edu/istmo/articulos/fin.html>.

Quevedo, Luis Alberto. "Política, medios y cultura en la Argentina de fin de siglo." *Los noventa. Política, sociedad y cultura en América Latina y Argentina de fin de siglo*. Ed. Daniel Filmus. Buenos Aires: Eudeba-Flacso, 1999. 201–24.

Rodríguez Villouta, Mili. *Cecilia querida. Historia de un amor improbable*. Buenos Aires: Planeta, 2001.

Schwartzenberg, Roger-Gérard. *The Superstar Show of Government*. New York: Barron's, 1980.

Sheines, Graciela. *Las metáforas del fracaso. Desencuentros y utopías en la cultura argentina*. Buenos Aires: Sudamericana, 1993.

Sklodowska, Elzbieta. *Testimonio hispanoamericano. Historia, teoría, poética*. New York: Peter Lang, 1992.

Solotorevsky, Myrna. *Literatura/Paraliteratura. Puig, Borges, Donoso, Cortázar, Vargas Llosa*. Gaithersburg, USA: Ediciones Hispamérica, 1988.

Steimberg, Oscar. *Semiótica de los medios masivos. El pasaje a los medios de los géneros populares*. Buenos Aires: Atuel, 1998.

Urbina, Nicasio. "La semiótica del testimonio: signos textuales y extra-textuales." *Istmo. Revista virtual de estudios literarios y culturales centroamericanos* 2 (2001) <http://www.wooster.edu/istmo/articulos/semiot.html>.

Van Den Heuvel, Pierre. *Parole, mot, silence. Pour une poétique de l'enonciation.* Paris: Librairie José Corti, 1985.

Van Dijk, Teun. *La ciencia del texto.* Barcelona: Paidós, 1992.

——. *Estructuras y funciones del discurso.* Madrid: Siglo Veintiuno, 1998.

Vázquez, Luciana. *La novela de Menem. Ensayo sobre la década incorregible.* Buenos Aires: Sudamericana, 2000.

Verbitsky, Horacio. *Robo para la corona. Los frutos prohibidos del árbol de la corrupción.* Buenos Aires: Planeta, 1991.

Verón, Eliseo. "Relato televisivo e imaginario social." *El espectáculo de la pasión. Las telenovelas latinoamericanas.* Ed. Nora Mazziotti. Buenos Aires: Colihue, 1993. 29–41.

Walger, Sylvina. *Pizza con champán. Una crónica de la fiesta menemista.* Buenos Aires: Espasa Calpe, 1994.

Wornat, Olga. *Menem. La vida privada.* Buenos Aires: Planeta, 1999.

——. *Menem-Bolocco S.A..* Buenos Aires: Ediciones B. Argentina, 2001.

Notes

[1] El esquema básico de la estructura argumentativa puede ejemplificarse con la secuencia "hipótesis-premisa-conclusión". En ella, el objetivo radica en "convencer al oyente de la corrección o la verdad de la aseveración, aduciendo suposiciones que la confirmen y la hagan plausible, o bien suposiciones a partir de las que pueda deducirse la aseveración" (Van Dijk, *Ciencia* 158). Por el contrario, la característica semántica fundamental en el caso de las estructuras narrativas radica en el hecho de que consisten en referir "acciones de personas, de manera que las descripciones de circunstancias, objetos u otros sucesos quedan claramente subordinados" (Van Dijk, *Ciencia* 154). Para mayores detalles en la descripción de las superestructuras que definirían uno u otro tipo de discurso véanse Van Dijk (1992 y 1998) y Jitrik (1995). Es verdad que, como señalan Ford y Longo, un texto narrativo, aunque carece de estructura argumentativa, "puede cumplir con el mismo propósito de la argumentación: dar origen a una interpretación y, frecuentemente, imponer una regla de acción" (132). En el caso de los textos que se presentan como de "investigación periodística" durante los noventa – y más tarde aún – en Argentina, toman como eje central la figura de un personaje destacado dentro de la sociedad argentina (generalmente un político, un empresario, un sindicalista) para terminar interpretando y generalizando sobre diversos aspectos de la realidad nacional. Lo interesante en este formato es ver cómo se termina recurriendo cada vez más a recursos retóricos "que no se corresponden con las exigencias de la documentación y la información" (Ford y Longo 134), jugando con la ambigüedad y la polisemia propia de los textos narrativos literarios o ficcionales.

[2] Para un acercamiento más completo al concepto de literatura testimonial, véanse Achugar (1992), Sklodowska (1992), De Grandis (1993) y Laforgue (2000). Pueden consultarse también Aguirre Aragón (2001), Córtez (2001), Mackenbach (2001), Nagy-Zekmi (2001), Pérez Cuadra (2001), y Urbina (2001).

[3] Así, la notoriedad de la figura pública y privada de Menem en la escena argentina aparecerá en *El jefe. Vida y obra de Carlos Saúl Menem*, de Gabriela Cerruti (1993), y en *Menem. La vida privada*, de Olga Wornat (1999). Las costumbres del entorno menemista serán analizadas en *Pizza con champán. Crónica de la fiesta menemista*, de Sylvina Walger (1994). Las peleas internas entre el binomio político Menem-Duhalde serán debatidas en *El*

otro. Una biografía política de Eduardo Duhalde, de López Echagüe (1996). El asesinato del periodista Cabezas, el posterior suicidio del empresario Alfredo Yabrán y su conexión con allegados al gobierno serán los temas de *Don Alfredo*, de Miguel Bonasso (1999). Mientras tanto, *Los dueños de la Argentina. La cara oculta de los negocios* (1992), *Los dueños de la Argentina II. Los secretos del verdadero poder* (1994) y *Los nuevos ricos de la Argentina. Tiburones al acecho* (1997), de Luis Majul, girarán alrededor de la vida de los empresarios relacionados con el poder político. Más recientemente, *Menem-Bolocco S.A.* (2001), de Olga Wornat otra vez, y *Cecilia querida. Historia de un amor improbable* (2001), de Rodríguez Villouta, tratarán de la boda del Dr. Menem con la chilena Cecilia Bolocco. No intentamos ser aquí exhaustivos. Para un lector interesado en más títulos relacionados con el tema, remitimos a Vázquez (228), en donde se podrá encontrar una muy completa bibliografía al respecto.

[4] Obsérvese la actitud pedagógica que en todo momento pretende Verbitsky desde su prólogo. Su objetivo será proveer al lector (al "ciudadano común", lo llama) con "herramientas informativas y analíticas" sobre la corrupción en Argentina, obtenidas a partir de diálogos privados con algunos implicados (9). Esto resulta importante de destacar, ya que la imagen pública y los discursos públicos (y que ocupan el centro de la escena) no son confiables (365). En *Robo para la corona*, el conflicto gira alrededor del desacuerdo con la palabra: un cuestionamiento al *status* de los documentos públicos y su interpretación a la luz de lo dicho en forma privada.

[5] El primero muestra en tapa y contratapa, y en fondo rojo, ángulos opuestos de un pastel de bodas. Éste, decorado con el signo "pesos" en cada uno de sus pisos, termina coronado con la clásica pareja de mazapán, pero esta vez con los rostros de Menem y su nueva esposa. Nombre de su autora y título aparecen marginados en el borde superior de las dos cubiertas, con una leyenda que le antecede: "Por la autora del bestseller *Menem: la vida privada*". Por otra parte, en la portada también puede percibirse, en forma vertical y en el borde izquierdo, una especie de "marca de agua" – solamente visible al ojo si no se mira el libro de frente – con la leyenda "Crónica actual" (nombre, posiblemente, de la colección).

[6] "Kitsch" es definido por Baudrillard como "a *pseudo-object*, which is to say as a simulation, copy, facsimile, or stereotype; as the paucity of true signification and as the overabundance of signs, allegorical references, or disparate connotations; as the exaltation of detail, and as the saturation by detail. Furthermore, there is a direct relationship between its internal organisation (a disconnected overabundance of signs) and its appearance in the market (a heaped mass of assorted objects. Kitsch is a *cultural category*" (75). Por su parte, Moles señala, entre los componentes del kitsch, "el amontonamiento, la sinestesia, la mediocridad ocasionalmente dorada, la ansiedad posesiva, la desproporción entre los medios y los fines, el romanticismo, un recuerdo del rococó, un toque del manierismo" (119) .

[7] Solotorevsky plantea una diferencia esencial entre folletín y novela rosa. Según esta autora, en el primero se percibe una "configuración de un mundo mayor, de intensidad épica y resonancia dramática" cuyo mensaje parece apuntar casi siempre a la difusión de ciertas ideas. La segunda, en tanto, presenta "la pintura de un mundo íntimo, sentimental, de tono menor", poniéndose siempre al servicio de las emociones en un nivel mucho más primario (43) .

[8] Obsérvese que la diagramación pareciera acercar el diseño de tapa a un afiche romántico, a un cuadro de fotonovela o, más aún, a un flirteo con el cómic. En este sentido, al "coqueteo" de tapa de los protagonistas y su posible diálogo, se añade el flirteo continuo con el doble sentido, con la indefinición genérica, con el artificio y la ilusión que el mismo texto propone. "Politics today is becoming a theater of illusion, and it is the spectator that

is under the illusion, diverted from real problems by the fascinating contemplation of a star actor giving vent to his emotions, some of which are sincere, others ficticious, and all egocentric. How can we deal with this sort of government show? How, except to echo André Malraux' phrase, 'To be a man is to reduce the amount of play-acting in one's life'" (Schwartzenberg 114).

Contributors

Guillermo Anad is a musician, writer, radio producer, and honourary research fellow in the Hispanic Studies Program, Monash University. He is the author of *Versos tomados* (2000) and his articles have appeared in *El Arca* (Buenos Aires) and *Antípodas* (La Trobe University). For Radio Nacional Argentina he produced the program *La Vuelta al Tango en Ochenta Mundos*.

Faye Bendrups is a theatre director, performance artist, composer, and has recently completed an extensive research project on Tango and Argentine identity for a PhD at La Trobe University. Her opera *Sindromtango: una ópera grotesca* has been produced to workshop stage in Buenos Aires and Melbourne. She is currently an honorary research fellow in the Hispanic Studies Program, Monash University.

Jeffrey Browitt is Senior Lecturer in Latin American Studies in the Institute for International Studies at the University of Technology, Sydney. He is the co-author with Andrew Milner of *Contemporary Cultural Theory* (Routledge, 2002) and has published articles on French Sociocriticism and Latin American literature and popular culture.

Kevin Foster teaches English at Monash University. He has published widely on representations of conflict in the Falklands and the Gulf, George Orwell, the Spanish Civil War, African autobiography, V. S. Naipaul, football and identity in Britain and Brazil. He is the author of *Fighting Fictions: War, Narrative and National Identity* (Pluto, 1999) and is currently completing a book on literary constructions of Latin America in Britain and America.

Hugo Hortiguera teaches Spanish at Griffith University, Brisbane. He was awarded his doctorate by the University of New South Wales with a thesis on the novels of the Argentine writer Osvaldo Soriano. He has published articles on contemporary Argentine literature and the teaching of Spanish as a foreign language in journals in the United States, Cuba, Israel and Argentina.

Stewart King teaches in Hispanic Studies at Monash University. He has published articles on Juan Marsé, Montserrat Roig, Manuel Vázquez Montalbán, Castilian-language writers from Catalonia, and Spanish crime fiction. His *Escribir la catalanidad. Lengua e identidades culturales en la* *narrative contemporánea de Cataluña* will be published in 2005 by Tamesis. He is currently editing a special number of *Antípodas* on narrative and cultural identity from Catalonia, the Basque Country and Galicia, and a collection on Castilian-language writers from Catalonia, which will be published by Editions Reichenberger (Kassel, Germany). He is presently working on a monograph on Spanish crime fiction.

Alfredo Martínez Expósito received his doctorate in Spanish Literature from the Universidad de Oviedo, Spain, with a thesis on Gómez de la Serna's theatre. Since 1993 he has lectured at the University of Queensland, Australia. His research topics include contemporary Spanish fiction, Spanish and Latin American film, and gender/sexuality in Spanish-speaking societies. He is the author of *Los escribas furiosos: configuraciones homoeróticas en la literatura española* (UP South, 1998) and has edited the collection *Gay and Lesbian Writing in the Hispanic World* (VOX/AHS, 2000).

Lilit Zekulin Thwaites teaches in the Spanish Program and is Deputy Dean of the Faculty of Humanities and Social Sciences at La Trobe University, Australia. Her research interests and publications focus primarily on aspects of contemporary Peninsular Spanish women's writing (prose and drama in particular) such as questions of identity, memory and the past; writing of/ from the periphery; female friendship; and literature as social commentary and criticism. These interests have led to her translating into English short stories by about a dozen women writers whom she has interviewed in Spain, with a view to publishing the translations as an anthology. Other projects currently underway include a study of the portrayal of older women in Spanish women's writing and film, and Latina writing.